T0334697

Cambridge Elements ≡

Elements in Publishing and Book Culture
edited by
Samantha J. Rayner
University College London
Leah Tether
University of Bristol

PRINTING TECHNOLOGIES AND BOOK PRODUCTION IN SEVENTEENTH-CENTURY JAPAN

Peter Kornicki
Robinson College, Cambridge

CAMBRIDGE
UNIVERSITY PRESS

Shaftesbury Road, Cambridge CB2 8EA, United Kingdom

One Liberty Plaza, 20th Floor, New York, NY 10006, USA

477 Williamstown Road, Port Melbourne, VIC 3207, Australia

314–321, 3rd Floor, Plot 3, Splendor Forum, Jasola District Centre,
New Delhi – 110025, India

103 Penang Road, #05–06/07, Visioncrest Commercial, Singapore 238467

Cambridge University Press is part of Cambridge University Press & Assessment,
a department of the University of Cambridge.

We share the University's mission to contribute to society through the pursuit of
education, learning and research at the highest international levels of excellence.

www.cambridge.org
Information on this title: www.cambridge.org/9781009495516

DOI: 10.1017/9781009495493

First published 2025

A catalogue record for this publication is available from the British Library

ISBN 978-1-009-49551-6 Paperback
ISSN 2514-8524 (online)
ISSN 2514-8516 (print)

Printing Technologies and Book Production in Seventeenth-Century Japan

Elements in Publishing and Book Culture

DOI: 10.1017/9781009495493

First published online: January 2025

Peter Kornicki

Robinson College, Cambridge

Author for correspondence: Peter Kornicki, pk104@cam.ac.uk

ABSTRACT: This Element first sets the history of printing in Japan in its East Asian context, showing how developments in China, Korea and elsewhere had an impact upon Japan. It then undertakes a re-examination of printing in seventeenth-century Japan, and in particular explores the reasons why Japanese printers abandoned typography less than fifty years after it was introduced. This is a question that has often been posed but never satisfactorily answered, but this Element takes a new approach, focusing on two popular medical texts that were first printed typographically and then xylographically. The argument presented here is that the glosses relied upon by Japanese readers could much more easily be provided when printing xylographically: since from the early seventeenth century onwards printed books customarily included glosses for the convenience of readers, this was surely the reason for the abandonment of typography.

KEYWORDS: typography, woodblock printing, Japan, moveable type, seventeenth century

ISBNs: 9781009495516 (PB), 9781009495493 (OC)

ISSNs: 2514-8524 (online), 2514-8516 (print)

Contents

1 Introduction 1

2 The East Asian Invention and Development of Typography 12

3 The Introduction of Typography to Japan 20

4 The Decline of Typography in Japan 34

5 Explaining the Decline of Typography 41

6 Two Early Seventeenth-Century Medical Texts 47

7 Takagi Takaaki's Argument 71

8 Conclusion 76

References 78

1 Introduction

Printing has a much longer history in East Asia than it has in Europe: that much is indisputable. It is a history that stretches back to the eighth century in the case of Japan and Korea, and most likely to the seventh century in the case of China. For a long time, the oldest evidence of East Asian printing traditions was thought to lie in Japan, where a very large number of Buddhist invocations (in Sanskrit, *dhāraṇī*) were printed between the years 764 and 770. From a European perspective, this is an astonishingly early date. Nevertheless, it is indeed in the eighth century that the history of printing in Japan begins.

At that stage the only writing system used in Japan was the Chinese system of graphs (characters). Therefore, those Buddhist invocations were printed using Chinese graphs alone. For the same reason, literate Japanese in the eighth century used Chinese graphs alone to write either in literary Chinese or in Japanese: there was no alternative option. Thus, for example, the Japanese poems contained in the eighth-century *Anthology of ten thousand leaves* (*Man'yōshū* 万葉集) were inscribed using Chinese graphs, for their sound values to represent Japanese words and inflections, for their semantic value to represent Japanese words of similar meaning or in other related ways. The cursive *hiragana* syllabary and the angular *katakana* syllabary, which are used to this day to write Japanese verbal inflections and grammatical particles, both emerged later, in the course of the ninth century. From that time onwards literate Japanese had the additional options of writing in Japanese using a mixture of Chinese graphs and one or other of the two syllabaries, or of using the syllabaries alone.

In this section I first discuss the antecedents of woodblock printing in East Asia, for the history of printing in Japan is intimately connected with developments in other parts of East Asia. Then I turn to seventeenth-century Japan and discuss the range of technologies available for the production of books.

First of all, let us consider how it was that large quantities of Buddhist invocations ever came to be printed in Japan in the eighth century. The invocations were extracted from a Buddhist text called the *Sutra of the dhāraṇī of pure unsullied light*. The original Sanskrit text of this sutra is no longer extant, but it had been taken from India to China, most likely in the seventh century, and there it had been translated into Chinese under the title *Wugou jingguang da tuouoni jing* 無垢浄光大陀羅尼経 (J. *Muku jōkō dai darani kyō*) by the year 705. The Chinese translation is known to have reached Korea in the year 706 and Japan at least by 737.[1] The invocations were extracted from it and in the 760s were printed in the capital, Nara; they were then rolled up one by one and placed inside miniature wooden pagodas. The pagodas were manufactured in Nara on lathes, which was then a new technology in Japan. Two workshops were established in Nara to undertake all this work, and although none of the printed invocations carries a date, some of the pagodas have an inscription on the base or another surface. For example, the pagoda in the Newberry Library in Chicago bears an inscription indicating that a man called 大田 (in modern Japanese this would be pronounced Ōta) made the pagoda on the twenty-eighth day of the fourth month of the second year of Jingo-Keiun (=768) in the Left Workshop (there were two workshops: a Left one and a Right one).[2]

Tens of thousands of these miniature pagodas and printed invocations survive to this day, both in Japan and elsewhere, and it is indeed possible, as the documentary sources record, that as many as one million were printed. These invocations are collectively known as the Hyakumantō darani (dhāraṇī of one million pagodas), and although printing on such a scale as early as the eighth century is truly astonishing, it is essential not to lose sight of two facts: firstly, this was indubitably a ritual act, and, secondly, the printed invocations were definitely not produced for the purpose of reading. After all, the texts were Sanskrit invocations written out using Chinese graphs for their sound value alone, so it is doubtful whether anybody in Japan could have read and understood them. The ultimate origins of this kind of ritual practice lay in Indian Buddhist practices, of which some

---

[1] Kornicki (2012), 50.

[2] The Newberry Library copy was purchased from Yamanaka & Co., Inc., New York, by Ernst Frederic Detterer (1888–1947), an American calligrapher and typographer who taught the history of printing at the School of the Art Institute of Chicago from 1921 to 1931. It was acquired by the Newberry Library in 1937.

archaeological traces survive and which were described in several sutras: these sutras were translated into Chinese in the seventh century and were then transmitted to other parts of East Asia in Chinese translation.[3]

Impressive though the Hyakumantō darani are, it is definitely not the case that printing was invented in Japan, although that claim has occasionally been made in the past. Nonetheless, nowhere in the world were any earlier examples of printing than the Hyakumantō darani known until 1966, when a startling find was made at the Pulguksa 佛國寺 temple in Kyŏngju in South Korea. The Sŏkkat'ap, a stone pagoda in the compound of the Pulguksa, was dismantled in that year and was found to contain a woodblock-printed copy of the *Sutra of the dhāraṇī of pure unsullied light*.

This is, of course, the same Buddhist sutra that contains the invocations printed in Japan, and, like the Japanese invocations, it includes some of the unorthodox characters introduced during the reign of Wu Zetian 武則天 (624–705), the only woman emperor of China, who ruled from 690 to 705. However, since these unorthodox characters continued to be used up to the ninth century, they cannot be taken as evidence that the sutra found in the Pulguksa was printed in the eighth century. Nonetheless, they do show that it was most likely printed before the year 900.[4]

The use of the same sutra in Japan and Korea is unlikely to be a coincidence. The *Sutra of the dhāraṇī of pure unsullied light* expounds the blessings and benefits that accrue from making multiple copies of the

---

[3] Kornicki (2012). There is no inventory of examples outside Japan, but there are several examples in the UK, including the British Museum (5), Cambridge University Library (4) and the National Library of Scotland (1), and in the USA, including Princeton University Library (2), Chicago University Library (1 without pagoda), the Newberry Library, Chicago (1), the Art Institute, Chicago (1), Yale University Library (4), the Metropolitan Museum of Art (1), the Minneapolis Institute of Art (1), the Library of Congress (1) and Columbia University (1). There are other examples in Germany (one each in the Stiftung Preußischer Kulturbesitz in Berlin; in the Gutenberg Museum in Mainz; in the Deutsches Buch- und Schriftmuseum, Leipzig; in the Deutsches Museum, Munich; and in the Bayerische Staatsbibliothek, also in Munich) and in France (one in the Bibliothèque Nationale in Paris).

[4] Tokiwa (1936); Drège (1984).

invocations contained within it and placing them inside miniature clay pagodas. Similar practices were recommended in other sutras which were translated into Chinese during the reign of Wu Zetian. These various translations are known to have been transmitted to Japan in the eighth century, and it is reasonable to assume that they had already been transmitted to Korea.[5] It seems likely, therefore, that the newly translated sutras from the court of Wu Zetian were transmitted both to Korea and to Japan and encouraged the ritual practices described therein. The *Sutra of the dhāraṇī of pure unsullied light* does not mention printing, but that was the technique used in Korea and Japan for the purpose of making multiple copies, although only one copy survives in Korea. It may well be that similar practices had been undertaken in China during the reign of Wu Zetian, but no evidence has yet come to light to support this hypothesis.

Since Korean records state that the Sŏkkat'ap pagoda had been sealed up in the year 751, it was evident, or so it was claimed, that the sutra found there must have been printed by that date. In fact, it has subsequently been shown that the pagoda had been opened on at least one occasion after 751. Nevertheless, there is widespread acceptance in Japan and in China, as well as in Korea, that this sutra was indeed printed in the eighth century at some point before 751. However, there is no documentary evidence whatsoever relating to printing in eighth-century Korea. As a result, it has been suggested by some Chinese and Japanese scholars that this sutra must actually have been printed in China and then been taken back to Korea by Korean monks or diplomats visiting China. The fact that the paper on which the sutra was printed is now known to be of Korean origin does not altogether rule that suggestion out of court, for Korean paper was frequently sent to China along with other tribute goods at this time. The Chinese scholar Pan Jixing has gone so far as to claim that the Korean copy of the *Sutra of the dhāraṇī of pure unsullied light* was in fact printed in Luoyang in 702, but he provides no evidence to support this claim. Unless new evidence comes to light, it is unlikely that this question will be definitively resolved. However, since Korea was in the eighth century a technologically more advanced society than Japan, it seems reasonable

[5] Kornicki (2012), 51–4.

to suppose that, if printing was undertaken in Japan in the 760s, it is all the more likely that it was already being practised in Korea.[6]

Although neither documentary sources nor archaeological finds have yet confirmed the prior development of printing in China, it is universally, and rightly, taken as given that the technology of woodblock printing developed there first and was subsequently transmitted to Korea and Japan.[7] This technology eventually gave rise in due course to a printed version of the Chinese translation of the *Diamond sutra*, of which a copy was found in the early twentieth century in Dunhuang, an important Silk Road settlement in north-west China. This printed version of the *Diamond sutra* bears a date corresponding to 868 and survives in just a single copy; what is more, it was printed not in the capital but in remote Sichuan province in south-western China and was subsequently taken to Dunhuang. Consequently, it is overwhelmingly probable that printing was already being widely practised in central China well before that time. Indeed, several Buddhist invocations, printed either in Sanskrit or Chinese, have been found in China that appear to be of greater antiquity than the *Diamond sutra*, but unfortunately none of them can be accurately dated. Doubtless the domestic warfare and the persecution of Buddhism that came at the end of the Tang dynasty (618–907) can be blamed for the destruction of most examples of early Chinese printing, and much else besides, but it is not out of the question that the archaeological investigation of tombs in and around the capital, Chang'an, may yet bring to light some texts printed in seventh-century China.[8]

The printing technology that was used in East Asia, both in these early centuries and, subsequently, right up to the twentieth century, was overwhelmingly woodblock printing or xylography. What kind of a technology is this? Woodblock printing is in fact a process that does not require special equipment and instead relies entirely on human labour and craft skills. It is, of course, not unique to East Asia. As early as the tenth century xylography was in use in what is now Egypt and elsewhere in the Middle East to print

---

[6] Pan (1997); Pan (2009), 216–17; Kornicki (2012).

[7] Barrett (2001a, 2001b, 2005, 2008, 2011); Kim (2000, 2007); Kornicki (2012).

[8] Seo (2003, 2009); Tsiang (2010), 233–7; Kornicki (2018), 109–14; Wood (2010).

amulets, pilgrimage certificates and the like, but it is not clear whether this was an independent development or was stimulated by knowledge of woodblock printing by the Uyghurs or in other parts of East Asia.[9] Further to the west, woodblock printing was also practised in Europe before Gutenberg's invention. Woodblock printing in Europe took the form of the woodcut, sometimes with text as well as an image. For example, a woodcut of St Christopher printed in southern Germany in 1423 contains two lines of text and is a particularly early example of a European woodcut with text.[10] In his classic account *The invention of printing in China and its spread westward*, which was first published in 1925, Thomas Carter claimed that the development of printing in Europe was connected with Asian printing traditions. Later writers, including Peter Burke and Joseph McDermott, have been unable to find any hard evidence to substantiate this claim, but recently Kristina Richardson has argued persuasively that the significance of the amulets printed in Egypt should be reconsidered, and she has put forward a new hypothesis concerning the antecedents to Gutenberg's printing activities.[11]

The woodblock-printing process as it was practised in East Asia is a simple one. The text to be printed was written on thin sheets of paper in uniform columns, usually by a professional scribe, and then the sheets were pasted face down onto a wooden block. The white parts were then cut away by skilled carvers, leaving the text and/or the lines of the illustrations raised from their surroundings. Printing was carried out by applying water-based ink to the upraised text and then impressing dampened paper onto the inked surface by hand. The woodblocks were usually approximately 45 centimetres wide, so this technology enabled a substantial section of text to be printed in a single operation. The *Diamond sutra* and other early printed

---

[9] Bulliet (1987); Schaefer (2006, 2014).

[10] On European woodcuts see Parshall and Schoch (2005). The German print of 1423 is held in the John Rylands University Library of Manchester and an image can be found here: https://bit.ly/4hl1rFh.

[11] Carter (1955); Burke and McDermott (2015); Richardson (2022), ch. 6 'A new narrative of premodern Afro-Eurasian printing'.

books were scrolls, so each section was printed separately and the sheets were then pasted together; the same technique was used for printing maps.[12]

From around the end of the first millennium, however, the codex (a number of leaves gathered together to create a book format) began to replace the scroll, and that shift resulted in a change in the way in which printing blocks were prepared. When printing was undertaken to produce books in the form of a codex, each folio (sheet containing two pages) was printed with a single block. Each sheet was printed on one side only: it was then folded in the centre with the text on the outside to produce a single leaf with text on both sides and, in the central fold (called the 'heart of the block', in Japanese *hanshin* 版心), an abbreviated title and the folio number. In the case of a full-page illustration covering the entire opening, half of the illustration would have to appear on the verso of one folio and half on the recto of the next – in other words, on the right half of one block and the left half of the next block – since East Asian books are read from right to left.[13]

It is important to be aware of the fact that since the text to be printed was written out by hand, woodblock printing is essentially a technology for the reproduction of handwriting, and the same can be said of the use of lithography for printing texts in Arabic, Persian and Urdu.[14] What is

[12] Suzuki, Tinios and Ruben (2013). The Korean sutra found in 1966 and the *Diamond sutra* were both indubitably printed with woodblocks. For some time, a theory held sway in Japan that the Hyakumantō darani were instead printed with metal plates, as explained by Hickman (1975). The argument was that woodblocks would have been incapable of printing the one million copies that, according to the documentary evidence, were printed and then distributed to ten temples. However, this takes no account of the fact that all the surviving printed *dhāraṇī* are connected with the Hōryūji temple in Nara. Multiple woodblocks could have been made to print the *dhāraṇī* supplied to the other nine temples thought to have received them. Consequently, the argument seems to me flawed. In any case, no evidence has been found to support the metal-plate theory, and it seems to have few supporters now.

[13] Suzuki, Tinios and Ruben (2013); Volker (1949).

[14] Davis and Chance (2016); Robb (2020), ch. 3 'Urdu lithography as a Muslim technology', 90–125.

more, it will be obvious from what has been said so far that woodblock printing (xylography) did not require the substantial capital investment that was required for the purchase of a printing press and founts of type in Europe. In East Asian xylography, the costs, apart from the paper and the ink, consisted of the purchase of the blank wooden blocks and the employment of the labour required to carry out the carving, printing, assembling and binding operations. Thus, the technology was portable and could be employed wherever the materials and labour could be found. It is for this reason that it was possible for the *Diamond sutra* to be printed in Sichuan, far from the Chinese capital, as early as the ninth century.

Up to this point my focus has been on the origins and early development of woodblock printing in East Asia as a whole. Let us now turn our attention to early seventeenth-century Japan. In the first half of the seventeenth century, three technologies for the production of books were in use in Japan at one and the same time. They were, in historical order of development, brush and ink on paper to produce manuscripts; woodblock printing or xylography, which had already been in use for hundreds of years; and moveable type printing or typography, which was first introduced to Japan in the 1590s. By the end of the seventeenth century one of those three technologies had fallen into disuse. Contrary to what might be expected, it was in fact the newest of those technologies – typography – that fell into disuse, even though in the West it is widely considered to be a more advanced printing technology than xylography. This perception of typography as superior is probably due to the fact that typography in the West was from the beginning a mechanical process owing to the invention of the manual printing press, while both xylographic and typographic printing in East Asia were unmechanised and relied solely on manual labour. However, it is an unwarranted assumption to consider typography as a more advanced technology, for in East Asian societies, at least, xylography proved more flexible and more commercially viable a technology than typography, all the way up to the nineteenth century.[15]

It goes without saying that, after the Meiji Restoration of 1868, which led to an influx of new technologies and ideas from the West, typography

---

[15] On this point, see Chow (2004).

in its more advanced nineteenth-century forms, including steam-powered presses, was adopted in Japan and xylography went into a decline from which it never recovered.[16] Thus, the second leg of the match between xylography and typography was decisively won by typography, but the first leg, in the seventeenth century, was equally decisively won by xylography.

My main aims in this Element are to consider what the impact of typography was on Japan in the seventeenth century, and to explain precisely why the first encounter was won by xylography. The question addressed here is therefore a simple one: why did Japanese publishers abandon the newly introduced technology of typography in the first half of the seventeenth century? In order to answer this question, I first consider the invention and spread of typography in East Asia and explain how it came about that typography was introduced to Japan in the 1590s. I then examine the data which shows a decline in the use of typography from the 1620s onwards and consider the merits of the various explanations which have so far been put forward. Finally, I present new evidence that suggests a different explanation and argue that the abandonment of typography in the seventeenth century can by no means be described as a technological step backwards to an inferior technology, but should instead be seen as a rational choice, one that makes good sense in the context of the time.

Before we consider the introduction of typography, however, we should absolutely not lose sight of the fact that the production of manuscript books in Japan continued right up to the end of the nineteenth century, notwithstanding the availability of two printing technologies. Although woodblock printing had triumphed by the middle of the seventeenth century and typography had dwindled into insignificance, manuscript production remained important, extensive and quantitatively significant until the early years of the Meiji period. This represents an easily overlooked continuity with the Kamakura (1189–1333) and

---

[16] Heijdra (2004a); Shockey (2019). On the transition and the early development of typography in Meiji Japan, see Suzuki (2022) and the other articles in issue no. 11 of the journal *Shomotsugaku* 書物学, which is devoted to Meiji typography.

Muromachi (1333–1600) periods. During those centuries domestic printing was mostly confined to Buddhist texts, and the demand for Chinese Confucian, literary and medical texts was met by precious imports from China, a small number of Japanese printed editions and numerous manuscripts copied in Japan. Texts written in Japanese, with a few exceptions, circulated – to the extent that they circulated at all – in manuscript alone. Consequently, it was manuscript traditions that kept the Japanese literary tradition alive until the principal texts were printed for the first time in the seventeenth century. It was then, in the seventeenth century, that the *Tale of Genji*, the *Record of the great peace* (*Taiheiki* 太平記), the *Pillow book of Sei Shōnagon* and other Japanese literary classics were printed for the first time, but by that time many other works had been lost, and they are now known to us only by their titles.[17]

In the Edo period virtually all the important literary texts of previous ages were printed. In spite of the fact that works such as the *Tale of Genji* and the *Tales of Ise* had been printed early in the seventeenth century, however, handwritten copies continued to be made. Printed editions could not compete with luxury copies that were written on fine paper by renowned calligraphers and often equipped with hand-painted illustrations, so for presentation at weddings and on other felicitous occasions it was manuscripts that were preferred. What is more, the act of copying had for many people in Edo-period Japan a significance that is difficult for us to grasp; in some cases, it arose out of an aversion to print; in others, it was a form of bodily learning, immersing oneself in a text by copying it out in its entirety. One of the best examples is furnished by Matsudaira Sadanobu 松平定信 (1787–1829), who was the de facto ruler of Japan from 1787 to 1794 and was then dismissed. In his retirement he made seven copies of the *Tale of Genji*, innumerable copies of the *Tales of Ise* and copies of several hundred other texts, all in his own hand. He appears to have found solace in copying texts, just like the eponymous heroes of Flaubert's last novel, *Bouvard et Pécuchet*.[18]

---

[17] Steininger (2018, 2019); Kornicki (2018), ch. 4 'Material texts: manuscripts, xylography and typography'.

[18] Ichinohe (2019); Miyagawa (2006); Okajima Ikuko (1997).

Other genres of manuscript production were abundant throughout the Edo period and rivalled print in quantity and variety. Fictionalised accounts of political scandals and other sensational events circulated widely, in spite of government prohibitions. Although in 1771 the booksellers' guild of Kyoto printed a list of the titles of such books with a warning to members of the guild that they should not under any circumstances handle them, it is all too clear that they continued to be sold in bookshops. Other clandestine manuscripts that could not be published included news digests and leaked copies of official documents. In addition, there were local histories and local school textbooks, which featured vocabulary and place names of local significance, collections of poetry, prose writings by women and writings recording 'secret traditions' (*hiden* 秘伝) and family teachings in many different areas of intellectual activity, including medicine.[19] It was by no means uncommon for printed books to be copied by hand if the original was rare or hard to obtain, or if the copyist lived in a remote area out of reach of bookshops and book pedlars. For example, the enlightenment pioneer of Meiji Japan, Fukuzawa Yukichi 福沢諭吉 (1835–1901), recalled in his autobiography that, in the 1850s and 1860s, students of Dutch, which was the only European language studied in Edo-period Japan, could earn good money by making copies of imported Dutch books for daimyo and other important personages who were eager to expand their knowledge of the West.[20]

Although the remainder of this Element will focus on the two print technologies which were in competition in the early seventeenth century, manuscript books continued to be produced in Japan for a variety of motives: they circulated just as widely as printed books, they were available for purchase in bookshops, and they could be borrowed for a fee from commercial circulating libraries (*kashihon'ya* 貸本屋). Manuscripts and printed books, therefore, occupied a shared space throughout the Edo period, as they did in many other supposedly 'print' societies elsewhere, including China and Korea.[21]

---

[19] Kornicki (2006).   [20] Fukuzawa (2007), 83–4.

[21] Magnússon (2017) provides a good survey of the field of manuscript studies in the age of print in East Asia and elsewhere. On manuscripts in China, see McDermott (2006).

2 The East Asian Invention and Development of Typography

There is no room for doubting that typography was invented in Song-dynasty China (960–1279) at least 400 years before Gutenberg's printing activities. It was invented by a person called Bi Sheng 畢昇 (990–1051), and the process was described by Shen Kuo 沈括 (1031–95) in his *Brush talks from a dream brook* (*Mengxi bitan* 夢溪筆談), which was completed in 1091. Shen records that 'When Pi [Bi] Sheng died, his fount of type passed into the possession of my nephews, and up to this time it has been kept as a precious possession', so there are good grounds for concluding that his account is genuine. At this stage typography seems to have been limited to the northern part of Zhejiang province, a little to the south of Shanghai.[22] And there is some good evidence to suggest that, under the inspiration of Shen Kuo's account, earthenware type was used to print books in China on two occasions in the thirteenth century. In the 1240s, for example, Yao Shu 姚樞 (1201–78) urged one of his followers to use 'Shen type' to print the writings of the Neo-Confucian philosopher Zhu Xi 朱熹 (1130–1200). Whether any printing resulted from this suggestion is unknown, but at the very least it is clear that knowledge of the technique developed by Bi Sheng and described by Shen Kuo had spread beyond Zhejiang province to other parts of China by this time. Needless to add, no books printed at that time have survived to the present day.[23]

On the other hand, we have a very precise account of the manufacture of wooden type in *Zao huozi yinshufa* 造活字印書法 (*The technique of making moveable type and printing books*), a work written in 1298 by Wang Zhen 王禎 (fl. 1290–1333), who served as a government official. Wang, who was an agronomist and inventor, also experimented with tin moveable type and clay type, but it was wooden type that he used for the purpose of printing books. These apparently included the *Jingde County Gazetteer* (*Jingde xianzhi* 旌德縣誌), which was printed in 1298, but again no copies have

---

[22] Tsien (1985), 202; Hu (2012), 130; Hu et al. (2008), 2: 550–3; Bussotti and Han Qi (2014), 14. For a critical survey of the various editions and translations of Shen Kuo's *Brush talks from a dream brook*, see Sivin (2015).

[23] Bussotti and Han Qi (2014), 15.

survived. In 1322 Ma Chengde 馬稱德 (d.1322), a local official in Zhejiang, made a large quantity of wooden type and apparently printed the *Compendium to the great learning* (*Daxue Yanyi* 大學衍義) in forty-three volumes. No copies of this survive either. On the other hand, it seems that one copy of the Yuan-dynasty *Dissertations for examination at the Imperial Palace* (*Yushice* 御試策), which was printed typographically probably between the years 1334 and 1368, is preserved in the National Library of China in Beijing. This appears to be the oldest extant Chinese typographic book and dates from about a century before Gutenberg.[24] However, as we will see, this is by no means the oldest extant typographic book in the world.

It is certain that wooden type was being used during the Ming (1368–1644) and especially the Qing (1644–1911) dynasties, and bronze type was being used to print some books in the last decade of the fifteenth century and the first decades of the sixteenth. In the last decades of the Ming dynasty wooden type was used to print a considerable number of titles, and more than 100 of these are extant in at least one copy. Later, in the Qing dynasty, there was a resurgence of interest in typography, and for the first time successive emperors took an interest in this alternative technology.[25]

Although it is beyond a shadow of a doubt that experiments with typography were indeed undertaken in China well before the time of Gutenberg, it is equally clear that typography did not take root in China until the eighteenth century and, as Bussotti and Han have noted, in China typography 'never challenged the dominance of xylography'. In view of the fact that typography was used extensively in Korea to print Chinese texts well before the eighteenth century (see later in this section), it is surprising that this was not the case in China. No satisfactory explanation for the contrasting lack of enthusiasm in China has yet been put forward, though it is clear that the kind of state support for typography that was forthcoming in Korea and in other East Asian societies was lacking in China.[26] That, of course, raises another question – namely, why

---

[24] Bussotti and Han Qi (2014), 18.

[25] Bussotti and Han Qi (2014), 21–3; Chow (2007), 190; Tsien (1985), 201–20; Zhang (2009), ch. 2; Inoue (2011), ch. 3. Chow's figure is based on Xiao Dongfa (1996), 343–4, but she points out that this is surely an underestimate.

[26] Bussotti and Han Qi (2014), 14 (quotation), 20–1.

there should have been no state support for typography in China until the Qing dynasty – but that is a question that lies beyond the scope of this Element.

What is equally surprising is that, within 100 years of Bi Sheng's invention, the new technology appears to have been transmitted to the Tangut empire, which ruled over what is now the Ningxia Hui Autonomous Region in north-central China. The Tanguts deserve to be better known than they are. They were a Sino-Tibetan people whose empire was destroyed by the Mongol empire in 1227. In Chinese scholarship the Tanguts and their empire are referred to as the Xi Xia 西夏 or 'Western Xia', but in Western and Russian scholarship they are now referred to by the name Tanguts, which derives from the Mongolian name for them; the Tanguts called themselves 'Mi-nia', or 'High and White'. Although much of the material culture of the Tanguts was destroyed by the Mongols following their invasion, in 1900 some Tangut texts were found during the Boxer Rebellion in China, and subsequent archaeological excavations in the ruins of the Tangut city of Khara-Khoto brought to light many more Tangut texts. Some of these texts were written in Tangut, a Tibeto-Burman language which was written in a logographic script like Chinese graphs that is thought to have been invented in 1036. Tangut uses more than 5,000 graphs, which at first glance seem similar to Chinese graphs but are in fact completely different. Other texts found in Khara-Khoto were in Chinese, or in a mixture of Tangut and Chinese.[27]

A substantial addition to the corpus of Tangut texts was made in 1990, when vandals destroyed a pagoda at Baisigou in the Ningxia Hui Autonomous Region and inadvertently revealed the existence of a hidden library. The books found here and in other archaeological investigations reveal that the Tanguts not only made extensive use of woodblock printing, but that they also used wooden moveable type and possibly also type made of baked clay. Amongst the typographic books is a copy of a Tangut translation of a Chinese Buddhist text titled *Jixiang bianzhi kouhe benxu* 吉祥遍至口合本續 (*Auspicious tantra of all-reaching union*): although it does not carry a date, it is considered to have been printed in the twelfth century. It is, therefore, the oldest book printed with

---

[27] Dunnell (1996).

moveable type so far discovered anywhere in the world.[28] How and when typography was transmitted from China to the Tangut empire is unknown; since the Tanguts maintained diplomatic relations with Song-dynasty China, there was a possible conduit in existence for the transmission of texts and technologies.[29] Again, why the Tanguts took so enthusiastically to a technology that had only a marginal presence in China is unclear, but the colophons of surviving examples of Tangut typography reveal that the state was actively involved in promoting printing with moveable type. The same was true of Korean typography, but in China the state appears to have given no encouragement to typography until the eighteenth century.[30] It is clear that the Tangut and Korean states perceived some advantage in the use of typography, but it should be noted that in neither society did typography displace xylography. Rather, the two technologies were used in tandem.

It was not only the Tanguts who acquired knowledge of typography and used the new technology to print books; the technology was also transmitted to the Uyghurs in Central Asia, to the Korean peninsula and to Vietnam – though exactly how the knowledge spread is unknown, for there is no documentary record to cast light on the process. With regard to the Uyghurs, in 1908 Paul Pelliot discovered nearly 1,000 pieces of Uyghur type in Dunhuang, all made of wood and engraved with words and phonetic groups of letters in the Sogdian script. It is not known when this wooden type was made, but it is thought to date from the twelfth or thirteenth centuries, when the Uyghurs were also actively using xylography to print books. To date, no Uyghur typographic books or fragments of them have been identified, but the pieces of type found by Pelliot show traces of ink, so there can be no doubt that they were used.[31]

---

[28] Galambos (2015); Sun (2007); Hou (2017); Drège (2006); Niu (2004).

[29] As Bussotti and Han Qi (2014) point out, the supposition that Shen Kuo himself may have during his military service passed the technology on to the Tanguts cannot seriously be entertained: 17.

[30] Bussotti and Han Qi (2014).

[31] Shi Jinbo and Yasen Wushou'er (2000), 87–110 and plates 30–1; Macouin (1986); Elverskog (1997), 10–11, 81; Bussotti and Han Qi (2014), 18.

In Vietnam, typography seems to have been practised on a rather limited scale. Chinese sources refer to typographic printing in Vietnam in the fifteenth century, but no examples have survived.[32] This is not surprising, for the written heritage of Vietnam has suffered huge losses as a result both of the Ming invasion of 1406 and of what in Vietnam is called the American War. We know, for example, that in 1435 the *Great collection of commentaries on the Four Books* (Ch. *Sishu daquan* 四書大全), which had been compiled in China twenty years earlier, was printed xylographically in Vietnam, but not a single copy survives; in fact, the oldest xylographically printed Vietnamese book dates only from the late seventeenth century.[33]

In the eighteenth century there seems to have been something of a revival of typography in Vietnam, which was probably due to the increased use of typography in China in the early eighteenth century. In 1773 the prominent Vietnamese scholar Lê Quí Đôn 黎貴惇 (1726–84) provided an account of typography that was presumably based on Chinese sources.[34] No typographic books printed in Vietnam appear to survive, but several xylographic facsimiles of typographic books are extant and, although few in number, they show that typography was indeed practised in Vietnam, albeit probably not extensively.[35]

It was on the Korean peninsula that typography was used more extensively and enthusiastically than anywhere else in East Asia. Typography was used to print books in Korea from at least the thirteenth century onwards, utilising both metallic and wooden moveable type.[36] The oldest extant book printed in Korea with metal type is the *Essential passages pointing directly to the mind: Writings compiled by the monk Paegun* (K. *Paegun hwasang ch'orok pulcho chikchi simch'e* 白雲和尙抄錄佛祖直指心體要節), which consists of texts assembled by Paegun 白雲 (1298–1374). This book, which is often referred to as the *Jikji*, was printed in 1377 in the Hŭngdŏksa 興德寺 temple in the southern part of the Korean peninsula, but only the final volume is extant, preserved in the Bibliothèque Nationale

[32] Liu Yujun (2005), 271.

[33] *Đại Việt sử ký toàn thư*, bản kỷ 11 (1435.12.11), in Chen (1984–6), 2: 591.

[34] Lê Quí Đôn (2011), 375–8. [35] Yamamoto (1999); Liu Yujun (2005), 271.

[36] Ch'ŏn (1976), 79–112, 123–7; Son (1987).

in Paris.[37] However, there are older pieces of Korean bronze type in existence, and, according to a preface written by Yi Kyubo 李奎報 (1168–1241), it seems that twenty-eight copies of a book on Confucian rites were printed with metal type in or around the year 1234 and subsequently distributed to government agencies. What is more, in 2010 some pieces of thirteenth-century type were found in Korea, and it is now widely accepted that these are the oldest pieces of Korean printing type so far found.[38] There is little room for doubting, then, that printing with metal moveable type was initiated in Korea in the thirteenth century, if not before.

When the long-lasting Chosŏn dynasty (1392–1897) was founded in 1392, the government created an Office for Books (*Sŏjŏgwŏn* 書籍院), which was responsible for printing and publishing books, and in 1403 King T'aejong 太宗 established a Type Casting Office (*Chujaso* 鑄字所), thus indicating a renewed state commitment to metal typography.[39] T'aejong announced that he desired to put typography to work for the benefit of the state:

> In order to govern the country well, it is essential that books be read widely … It is my desire to cast copper [bronze] type so that we can print as many books as possible and have them made available widely. This will truly bring infinite benefit to us.[40]

In the course of the fifteenth century, a total of seventeen different founts of type were cast and four founts of wooden type were carved as well, all for government printing initiatives.[41] Before the invention of the Korean alphabet, the type naturally consisted only of Chinese graphs, but from 1447 onwards they included the Korean alphabet, *han'gŭl*, to make vernacular printing possible. Since the individual letters of the *han'gŭl* alphabet are combined in various ways and different shapes to form syllabic blocks – for example, the letters *h* ㅎ, *a* ㅏ and *n* ㄴ are combined to form the syllable

---

[37] Son (1987), 149, 254–5.   [38] Kim (2013).

[39] *Chosŏn wangjo sillok*, T'aejo 1[1392].7.28, T'aejong 5[1403].2.13; Choi (2014), 141; Ch'ŏn (1976), 79–112, 123–7.

[40] Lee, P. H. (1993–6), 1: 537.   [41] Son (1987), 151–9.

han 한 – each piece of *han'gŭl* type represented a whole syllable rather than the individual letters. From that time onwards, both typographic and xylographic books in Korea were printed either in Chinese graphs alone or in a combination of graphs and *han'gŭl*. An early example of a typographic book combining the two scripts is *Correct rhymes for Korea* (K. *Tongguk chŏng'un* 東國正韻), which was printed in 1448.[42]

From the account I have given, it will be apparent that typography had been practised in China, Korea, Vietnam, the Tangut empire and probably even Uyghur society long before it was ever introduced to Japan. Can this be right? Japanese monks and merchants were frequent visitors to China: is it possible that they were unaware of typography? Similarly, the *Annals of the Chosŏn dynasty* (*Chosŏn wangjo sillok* 朝鮮王朝實録) reveal the frequent presence in Korea of emissaries from various parts of Japan, and many of them requested books, usually the second edition of the Korean Buddhist canon, which was completed in 1249, but occasionally other items in addition.[43] Were they, too, unaware of the typography practised in Korea? It is indisputable that a number of Korean books reached Japan in the fifteenth and sixteenth centuries, but so far it has not proved possible to demonstrate that any Korean typographic books reached Japan before 1590. The one possible exception is part of a copy of the Chinese chronicle the *Book of Han* (*Hanshu* 漢書), which was printed in Korea with moveable type in 1431 and which is preserved in the library of Bukkyō University in Japan. The postface of this edition, which is dated 1428, refers explicitly to the casting of (metal) type and the benefits of this invention for the dissemination of texts, so it should have been obvious to careful readers that this was not a xylographic book. But the question still to be answered is when exactly this book reached Japan. According to Japanese scholar Hiranaka Reiji, this copy of the *Book of Han* contains abundant handwritten *kunten* glosses (which enable Japanese readers to translate literary Chinese texts into Japanese) and other annotations, and he states that these are thought to be the work of a Kyoto monk of the Muromachi period.[44] If that is true, it is possible that this book reached Japan in the sixteenth century, or even in the late fifteenth century, but there is no certainty to be had about the date of its arrival or that

---

[42] Son (1987), 274–5; Lee Hee-Jae (1987). [43] Kornicki (2013).

[44] Hiranaka (1967), 467.

of the annotations. It would certainly be surprising if no Korean typographic books whatsoever had reached Japan before 1590, but the inescapable fact remains that there is no mention of Korean typography in Japanese sources before then, nor is there any sign of Japanese awareness of typography until the very end of the sixteenth century.

It is hard to believe that Japanese envoys did not come across typographic books in Korea, unless there was a determined effort to keep the technology secret, but there is no sign of any such efforts in the *Annals of the Chosŏn dynasty*. It may be that visiting Japanese did in fact see typographic books but did not appreciate that they were produced using a different technology from xylography; alternatively, they may have regarded the new technology as of no interest. Whatever the case, there is no mention of Korean typography in Japanese sources until after 1592, when Toyotomi Hideyoshi, the de facto ruler of Japan, launched an invasion of the Korean peninsula. As a by-product of the invasion, not only were Korean typographic books taken to Japan in large quantities but also founts of metal and wooden type.[45] Consequently, unless it can be demonstrated that Japanese were aware of Korean moveable type before 1592, it seems indisputable that it was in fact European typographic technology that reached Japan first, in 1590.

Nevertheless, what is undeniable is that a large number of books were looted during the invasion of Korea and taken to Japan during the years 1592 to 1598. Amongst them were many Korean typographic editions of Chinese texts, and, as a result, there were in Japan in the 1590s very many more Korean typographic editions than European typographic editions. And the Korean editions had a lasting influence, for in the first half of the seventeenth century a number of them were reprinted in Japan in xylographic facsimile editions. These editions relied upon a procedure known as *kabusebori* 被せ彫り, whereby an existing book is dismantled and the individual printed pages are pasted onto woodblocks for carving. Facsimiles produced in this way reproduce all the features of the original, often including the original colophon, but in Japan *kunten* reading glosses were usually added to the Chinese text by hand before the pages were pasted onto the blocks for carving.

---

[45] Kawase (1967a), 1: 151–2, 178.

3 The Introduction of Typography to Japan

The printing technology in use in Japan up to the 1590s was the only one known to Japanese in the preceding centuries, namely xylography or woodblock-printing. In the 1590s, however, typography was introduced to Japan for the first time, and for several decades the new technology was taken up with enthusiasm not only by the imperial household and by successive shoguns but also by individuals and some commercial publishers. Much significance has been attached to this phenomenon, as the following quotation shows:

> Despite these editions being quickly replaced once more by woodblock printing, their contribution to broadly acquainting people with the value and power of printing cannot be over-estimated. Without this seminal period in the development of commercial publishing, the multi-faceted cultural development of the Tokugawa [Edo] period would have been unthinkable.[46]

Can this really be true? Can it be that a technology that was soon discarded, as the first phrase acknowledges, had such an important role? Would later developments really have been unthinkable without this brief dalliance with typography? There is a suspicion that the appeal and mystique of Japanese typography has generated a somewhat exaggerated sense of its importance in the history of the book in Japan.

The source of the new technology in Japan was twofold: European missionaries on the one hand, and Korea on the other. The European tradition of typography, which originated with Gutenberg in the middle of the fifteenth century, reached Japan in 1590 when the Italian Jesuit missionary Alessandro Valignano (1539–1606) brought a printing press to Japan. This was used by the Jesuits in Kyūshū to print a variety of works, but most of the items printed were for the use of the Jesuit missionaries themselves and were therefore either devotional works or books to help them with their studies of Japanese. They included an extract from the *Tale of the Heike* (*Heike monogatari* 平家物語),

---

[46] Sasaki (2022), 28.

which was in fact the first work of Japanese literature ever to be printed, although it was printed in a transcription in Roman script rather than in Japanese script. Owing to the suppression of Christianity in Japan in the early seventeenth century, few of the imprints of the Jesuit mission press have survived, and those that have survived are mostly extant in a single copy.

It is unclear how widely these Jesuit editions circulated, for almost all of them were printed in Kyūshū, far from the centres of power in Japan. Although these books were produced by the Jesuits for their own use and were not for sale or distribution, some may have reached other hands, as is suggested by a letter that the Rev. Patrick Copland, minister of a church in Bermuda, wrote in 1639 to John Winthrop, governor of the Massachusetts Bay Colony. In the letter Copland states that he had visited Nagasaki, adding that 'These I had of Capt. Cox [i.e., Richard Cocks], our Cape-merchant [i.e., head merchant], a Popish catechism imprinted in Naugesack [Nagasaki], in the Italian letter, and Japan tongue, which catechism I have now in my study.' Copland, who was a Presbyterian, had joined the East India Company as chaplain on its tenth voyage in 1612; the ships taking part reached Bantam (now Banten in Java, Indonesia), where they remained for a while and one of them, the *Hosiander*, sailed on to Japan in 1615, with Copland on board. Richard Cocks, the head of the English Factory in Japan, certainly met Copland, for he mentions him in his diary. It appears from Copland's account that Cocks had acquired a Jesuit imprint, which seems to have been a Japanese text in Roman script. Since Copland is thought to have left Japan in 1620, Cocks must have acquired it before that, perhaps on a visit to Nagasaki. At any rate, Copland's letter shows that at least some of the Jesuit imprints did reach other hands.[47] It is not known if Jesuit imprints ever reached the eyes of Japanese intellectuals unconnected with the Christian missions, although the Jesuit Collegio (seminary) in Kyoto might have provided opportunities for Jesuit imprints to be seen by a wider audience.[48] However, we now know that the Jesuit imprints were not hermetically confined to their own community, so some of them probably did reach Japanese hands.

---

[47] Copland (1639), 278–9; Farrington (2001), 158; Tōkyō Daigaku Shiryō Hensanjo (1978–80), vol. 3: 4; Farrington (1991), 168 n. 1, 1552.
[48] Loureiro (2006); Moran (1993); Tenri Toshokan (1973).

As I explained in the previous section, the Korean tradition of typography had a history of several centuries by the time it reached Japan, and its arrival seems to have been entirely due to Hideyoshi's invasion of Korea. As a result, within the space of just two years two different traditions of typography had reached Japanese shores. These two traditions were put to work in Japan in very different contexts. Down in Kyūshū, far from the capital, the Jesuits printed a number of books for their own use or for that of Japanese converts, beginning in 1591 and ending in the second decade of the seventeenth century, when the persecution of Christianity intensified. Some of the Jesuit imprints were in Latin but others were in Japanese, either in Roman transcription or in Japanese script. The oldest extant item is a single sheet containing Japanese translations of the Lord's Prayer, the Apostles' Creed and other prayers, which was printed with cursive Japanese type representing *hiragana* syllables. This is thought to have been printed in late 1590 or 1591. At any rate, in 1591 the Jesuits also printed the *Dochiriina Kirishitan* (Christian doctrine) and other works in Japanese script, so it is clear that, soon after the acquisition of a printing press, the Jesuit missionaries in Kyūshū were printing in Japanese using freshly carved wooden type.[49]

Meanwhile, in the capital, Kyoto, typographic printing began in 1593, the very year after Hideyoshi launched the invasion of Korea. In that year a fount of metal moveable type taken from Korea was presented to Emperor Go-Yōzei 後陽成, and on his instructions the old text of the *Classic of filial piety* (*Gu wen Xiao jing* 古文孝経, J. *Kobun Kōkyō*) was printed. A brief description of the printing process survives in a courtier's diary, and this provides some details. It appears from the diary that twelve men in the entourage of Go-Yōzei began working towards the end of the ninth month of 1593, using a fount of metal type recently imported from Korea, and completed the process two months later. However, possibly because the quantity of copies printed was very small, there is no further record of any copies of this book and no copy has yet come to light. Another possibility is that the printers did not appreciate the need for an ink that would adhere to

---

[49] The most accurate and up-to-date list of the Jesuit imprints in Japan, together with images, is to be found in the Kirishitan Bunko database (https://digital-archives.sophia.ac.jp/laures-kirishitan-bunko/).

metal, with the result that the printed text was of poor quality. Be that as it may, Go-Yōzei subsequently sponsored the printing of other works, including, in 1597, the anthology of Chinese poetry *Brocade of embroidered verse* (*Kinshūdan* 錦繡段) and an anthology of Chinese prose and verse titled *Texts encouraging study* (*Kangakubun* 勧学文). The postfaces of both of these books assert that the printing technique used, which required Chinese graphs to be chiselled out of wood one by one, had recently been transmitted from Korea.[50] This makes it clear that wooden type as well as metal type must have been imported from Korea.

Before these two works had been printed by Go-Yōzei in 1597, the monk Niho 日保 of the Honkokuji 本圀寺 temple in Kyoto had printed the *Preface to the profound meaning of the lotus sutra* (J. *Hokke gengi jo* 法華玄義序) and the *Commentaries on the outline of the Tiantai fourfold teachings* (J. *Tendai shikyōgi shūge* 天台四教儀集解). Since these were both printed towards the end of 1595, they are now the oldest extant books printed typographically by Japanese, but, as we have seen, the Jesuit missionaries had in 1591 already printed several books that are still extant. The colophon of the *Preface to the profound meaning of the lotus sutra* indicates that 100 copies were printed, and in fact many copies have survived to the present day. The *Preface* and the *Commentaries* both seem to have been printed using wooden moveable type, but it is unclear how the Honkokuji temple came to be involved in typography so quickly. Kawase notes that the temple belongs to the Nichiren school of Buddhism and speculates that the temple may have had some connection with Katō Kiyomasa 加藤清正, who was one of the three senior commanders during the invasion of Korea and was a fervent follower of Nichiren Buddhism. It is possible that he provided the Honkokuji monks with some wooden type from Korea, but this is a matter of speculation not fact.[51]

In the following year (1596), an individual named Oze Hoan 小瀬甫庵 (1564–1640) began to undertake printing. He was both a physician and a scholar of Confucianism, and most of the works he published were Chinese medical texts, including *The fourteen bodily tracts explained* (*Shisijing fahui* 十四經發揮, J. *Jūshikei hakki*) in 1596 and *The new edition of the true*

---

[50] Kawase (1967a), 1: 152–4, 177–97, 255–328, 329–36; Sasaki (2022), 31–2.

[51] Kawase (1967a), 1: 154–5, 3: 18.

transmission of medicine (*Xinbian yixue zhengzhuang* 新編醫學正傳, J. *Shinpen igaku seiden*) in 1597. Oze Hoan is thought to have served as the personal physician to Toyotomi Hidetsugu (1568–95), the nephew of Hideyoshi, and it may have been his proximity to power that enabled him to gain access to the newly imported technology of typography so quickly.[52]

In 1598 Hideyoshi's life came to an end and the Japanese armies withdrew from the Korean peninsula. In the following year, Tokugawa Ieyasu (1543–1616) began to show an interest in typography. In 1600 Ieyasu was to emerge victorious from the Battle of Sekigahara, and in 1603 to inaugurate what is now known as the Tokugawa shogunate, but in 1599 he ordered 100,000 pieces of wooden type to be carved. With these he had several works printed in Fushimi, to the south of Kyoto, including the Japanese historical chronicle *Mirror of the East* (*Azuma kagami* 吾妻鏡) and a number of Chinese military, administrative and Confucian texts which had never before been printed in Japan.[53]

Also in 1599, the *Guide to prolonging life* (*Enju satsuyō* 延寿撮要) was written and printed by Manase Gensaku 曲直瀬玄朔 (1549–1631). This was the first work to be printed in Japan immediately after its composition, and it may well have been written with printed distribution in mind. The significance of this work lies in the fact that the Manase family was committed to making medical knowledge accessible through use of the vernacular. Consequently, the *Guide* was printed in Japanese using *hiragana* wooden type. In order to replicate the normal cursive use of the *hiragana* script, Manase Gensaku had a number of ligatures carved which combine two, or sometimes three, *hiragana* letters, as can be seen in Figure 1.

During the first two decades of the seventeenth century, typography dominated printing activity in Japan. This is obvious from the statistics of extant imprints tabulated in Figure 3 in Section 4. Xylography was responsible for fewer titles than typography in those two decades, but it should be emphasised that these statistics relate to titles and there is no way of knowing the number of copies printed. All the same, the domination of typography in early seventeenth-century Japan needs to be emphasised; it

---

[52] Kawase (1967a), 1: 155–9.

[53] Kawase (1967a), 1: 211–17. On the choice of books, see Kornicki (2008), 74–6.

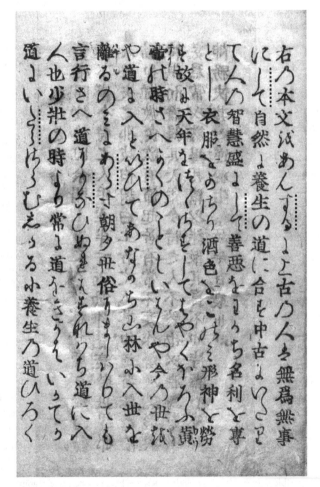

Figure 1 Typographic edition of *Guide to prolonging life* (*Enju satsuyō*) printed in 1599 (unpaginated; f.1b). I have indicated some of the ligatures with dotted lines to the right. National Archives of Japan.

may have been short-lived, but it does not seem to have a parallel in East Asia, except possibly Korea.[54] It is for this reason that I use the word 'reversion' when referring to the subsequent revival of xylography from the third decade of the seventeenth century onwards, for many printers who had started their activities with typography turned back to xylography later.

What accounts for the domination of typography in Japan, brief though it was? As many have suggested, it may possibly have been a result of the example shown by Emperor Go-Yōzei from 1593 onwards, by Go-Yōzei's successor, Emperor Go-Mizunoo 後水尾 and by Tokugawa Ieyasu, who became the shogun in 1603. Go-Mizunoo commissioned the printing of the *Categorised garden of the empire* (*Huangchao leiyuan* 皇朝類苑, J. *Kōchō ruien*), which was printed in 1621. This was a substantial encyclopedia completed in China in 1145 during the Song dynasty; it has long been thought that the Japanese edition was printed with metal type, but it may in fact have been printed with wooden type. Tokugawa Ieyasu, too, continued to be interested in typography. Just before he retired to Sunpu (now Shizuoka) in 1607, he ordered that more than 100,000 pieces of bronze type be cast, and of these some 38,000 pieces survive.[55] This fount of type was used in 1616 to print the *Essentials of governance based on ancient writings* (*Qunshu zhiyao* 群書治要, J. *Gunsho chiyō*), which is a political encyclopedia originally compiled in China in the early seventh century.

Ieyasu did not live to take the printed copies of the *Essentials of governance based on ancient writings* in his hands, for he died in 1616. Surviving copies show that the particular requirements of printing with metal type had by this time been overcome: the water-based ink used for xylography and for printing with wooden moveable type will not adhere to a metal surface, but the clear impression of the text of the 1616 edition of *Essentials of governance based on ancient writings* shows that this problem had

[54] It is possible that there were periods in Korean history when typography dominated, but the statistics for typographic and xylographic imprints have yet to be compiled.

[55] The type can be seen at the Insatsu Hakubutsukan (Printing Museum) in Tōkyō; for an image, see www.printing-museum.org/en/collection/looking/15170.php.

been solved. However, because the printing was undertaken in some haste, there are a number of typographical errors, which were corrected in the xylographic edition of 1787.[56]

While the imperial court and the shoguns continued to sponsor printing in the early seventeenth century, other agents were rapidly taking up typography as well, including Buddhist temples. For centuries Buddhist temples had been at the forefront of printing in Japan, but they had mostly printed Buddhist texts of one sort or another and they had, of course, exclusively relied upon xylography. As mentioned, the Honkokuji temple in Kyoto printed two Buddhist books in 1595, and subsequently more than a dozen other temples took up typography as well. One of the few contemporary records we have is a diary kept by the court noble Funabashi Hidekata 舟橋秀賢 (1575–1614). This documents typographic printing activities on Mt. Hiei to the north-east of Kyoto between 1604 and 1607. The texts printed were either from the Chinese canonical tradition or Buddhist texts in Chinese, and it appears that the printers borrowed manuscripts from Funabashi Hidekata in order to establish a reliable text to print.[57]

One of the first temples to take up typography after the Honkokuji was the Yōhōji 要法寺 in Kyoto, where the monk Nisshō 日性 (1554–1614, also known as Enchi 円智) printed several works from 1600 onwards. Nisshō himself edited some of the texts and in other cases, such as the *Comparative chronology of the imperial lines of descent of Japan and China* (*Wakan kōtō hennen gōunzu* 倭漢皇統編年合運図) printed in 1600, he himself wrote the text. This was one of the first texts written in Japan precisely in order to be printed, and it seems to have been much in demand as a number of different editions were printed in a short space of time. This is an important point, for it is sometimes said that typography in East Asia was mostly used to print small numbers of copies. As we will see later, this was not necessarily true of Japan in the early seventeenth century.

---

[56] Kornicki (2008), 75. See the copy of the *Essentials of governance based on ancient writings* in the National Archives of Japan (https://bit.ly/4f4q9rF) and the entry for the copy in the British Library in Gardner (1993).

[57] Ueda (2023).

The *Comparative chronology of the imperial lines of descent of Japan and China* was the first of several non-Buddhist texts printed by Nisshō, and it is worthy of note that, departing from the tradition of Buddhist printing, in 1605 he also printed the *Age of the gods* (*Jindai no maki* 神代巻), which is the first part of the *Chronicles of Japan* (*Nihon shoki* 日本書紀), and the *Record of the great peace* (*Taiheiki*); at about the same time he also printed the *Collected commentaries on the Analects* (*Lunyu jijie* 論語集解, J. *Rongo shikkai*). Other temples, too, when undertaking typography, showed a greater interest than in previous centuries in printing both non-Buddhist works in Chinese and works of Japanese authorship. For example, the Honnōji 本能寺 temple in Kyoto printed the *Book of the Former Han* (*Qian hanshu* 前漢書, J. *Zenkanjo*) in twenty-five volumes in 1628.[58]

Amongst the other new agents taking up typography were physicans such as Oze Hoan and Manase Gensaku, who have both already been mentioned, and Baiju 梅寿, who will be discussed in Section 6. A particularly important new development was the emergence of publishers who printed not only non-Buddhist works in Chinese but also works in Japanese using the *hiragana* or *katakana* syllabaries. One of the earliest examples was the *Guide to prolonging life* (*Enju satsuyō*), which was printed in 1599 (Figure 1). The names of many of these individual publishers are recorded in the colophons of the books they published, and it is clear that some of them, at least, were commercial publishers. Take, for example, the case of Hon'ya Shinshichi 本屋新七, who printed the second part of the Chinese anthology *True treasury of old writing* (*Guwen zhenbao* 古文真實, J. *Kobun shinpō*) in Kyoto in 1609: his name indicates that he was a bookman by trade. There is in fact no evidence of a book trade of any kind in Japan before 1600, but it is evident that by the first decade of the seventeenth century the commerce of the book was beginning to lay down roots, and that in Kyoto the first commercial publishers were taking to typography. This tendency grew in the second and third decades of the seventeenth century, when more and more publishers turned either to the classics of Japanese literature or

[58] Kawase (1967a), 1: 255–77, 281.

to newly written fictional and other works in Japanese. Here, too, the notion that typography was only used for very limited editions sits uncomfortably with the use of typography by commercial publishers in the first few decades of the seventeenth century.

Amongst the most remarkable typographic productions of the first two decades of the seventeenth century are the so-called Sagabon 嵯峨本. They are said to have been the products of close collaboration between the wealthy merchant Suminokura Soan 角倉素庵 (1571–1632) and the famous craftsman and calligrapher Hon'ami Kōetsu 本阿弥光悦 (1558–1637), but little is known for sure, and in recent years the role of Kōetsu has been questioned. It is because they were printed in the Saga district in western Kyoto that they are known today as Sagabon (Saga books), but documentation is sparse and many questions remain. Although the output was limited in terms of number of titles, many were luxury editions, printed on high-quality coloured paper decorated with mica; they also made lavish use of ligatures to represent the flow of Japanese calligraphy. The texts printed in Saga included such classics as the *Tales of Ise* (*Ise monogatari* 伊勢物語), *Essays in idleness* (*Tsurezuregusa* 徒然草) and *An account of My Hut* (*Hōjōki* 方丈記), a digest of the *Tale of Genji* (*Genji kokagami* 源氏小鏡) and some chanting texts of Noh plays. They were all in Japanese, not Chinese, and none had ever been printed before (Figure 2). The first work to be printed was the *Tales of Ise* in 1608, though Koakimoto Dan has recently suggested that some other works that are not generally considered to be Sagabon were printed a year or two earlier in the same workshop. There are two important points that need to be drawn attention to here. One is the fact that, although most of the Sagabon were indeed printed typographically, a few of the titles were only printed in xylographic editions. The other is that at least ten different versions of the typographic edition of the *Tales of Ise* have so far been identified. Furthermore, in the 1620s, xylographic editions of the *Tales of Ise* were printed using coloured but not decorated paper. These two facts suggest that the type had constantly to be reassembled in the printing frames to print more copies, which in turn implies that the printers failed to anticipate demand. Again, we see that typography was not necessarily limited to the production of small numbers of copies. Similarly, the existence of the xylographic editions suggests that

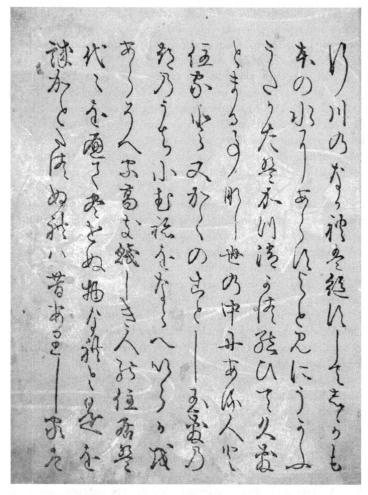

Figure 2 Undated Sagabon edition of *An account of My Hut* (*Hōjōki*) printed on paper patterned with mica (unpaginaged; f.1a). National Institute for Japanese Literature.

the printers finally abandoned typography for xylography.[59] These are both important points, and we will return to them later for further consideration.

It has long been taken for granted that the typographic boom in early seventeenth-century Japan was entirely a result of the importation of Korean typographic technology. After all, the earliest references to typography in Japan, which are to be found in the postfaces to the two works commissioned by Emperor Go-Yōzei, as mentioned earlier, ascribe the introduction of the technology to Korea and make no mention of the technology introduced by the Jesuits. However, from the early years of the twentieth century the scholar Shinmura Izuru began writing of the possibility that Jesuit printing had had an impact upon Japanese *hiragana* printing. This view developed greater traction in the 1980s and 1990s, when it was argued that Japanese printing practices were closer to European than to Korean practices, but other scholars remained unconvinced and the debate has continued without resolution.[60]

The latest contribution to the debate has been made by Sasaki Takahiro. He first provides a concise summary of the debate so far and frankly accepts that early Japanese typography undoubtedly had some features in common with Korean typography. These include the creation of ligatures combining two or more Chinese graphs, the use of embossing to create patterned covers (this became a standard feature of Japanese printed books of all kinds from the early seventeenth century onwards) and, in particular, the flower-petal and fishtail design appearing in the central fold of each page.[61] On the other hand, in terms of size, binding technique and the colours of the covers, Japanese typographic books clearly differed from Korean typographic editions from the outset, for Korean books tended to be large in size, to have a stitched binding using five holes (rather than the four which was common in Japan) and to have yellow covers.

Sasaki draws particular attention to the difference between Japanese typographic editions printed predominantly in *hiragana* and all other books

---

[59] Koakimoto (2021); Kinoshita (2000).

[60] Sasaki (2016). For a valuable summary of the debate, see Sasaki (2022), 34–9. See also Ōuchida (2009) for a lengthy discussion of some of the technical issues.

[61] Sasaki (2016) and Sasaki (2022), 62–4.

previously printed in East Asia. He argues that Japanese typography did indeed owe something to European typography, particularly the books printed in Japanese by the Jesuits. He accepts that 'there exists no firm evidence' that those who undertook to produce typographical editions of works in *hiragana* ever saw any of the books printed in Japanese script by the Jesuits. It is certainly true that the Jesuits printed an edition of *Contemptus Mundi* in Japanese script in Kyoto in 1610, and that may have been a point of contact between European and Japanese typography. However, by that time both the *Essays in idleness* and the *Tales of Ise* had been printed in Saga, so there must have been earlier points of contact if the Jesuit editions really did have an impact on Japanese *hiragana* typography.[62]

There is a further possibility, and that is that some of the Japanese who were involved in the Jesuit printing enterprises passed on some of their knowledge and experience. In a letter that Diogo de Mesquita (1551–1614), who was the Rector of the College of Nagasaki, wrote on 28 February 1599 to Claudio Acquaviva, the Superior General of the Society of Jesus in Rome, he referred in some detail to the printing process being used in Japan, including the use of Japanese paper. More importantly, he made it clear that Japanese brothers and acolytes were involved in the printing process:

> Here [Nagasaki] we have installed and put in order a very big and good printing press, on which we print books in Latin and others in the language and characters [graphs] of Japan, for which here, with our Brothers and *dōjiku*, we have carved two thousand punches and the same number of matrices, which are very exquisite because the Japanese are men of great ingenuity and skills.[63]

It is evident from this passage that a number of Japanese were intimately involved in the Jesuit printing process. It is possible, therefore, that one or more of them may have communicated details of the process or even shown

---

[62] Sasaki (2022), 70.

[63] González-Bolado (2023), 44. For the translation of *dōjiku* as 'acolyte', see note 15 of the same article.

an example of a typographic book to outsiders. This is of course pure speculation, but there has been no suggestion that the Jesuits sought to keep their printing technology secret in Japan, so some form of technology transfer was certainly possible. And, as we have seen earlier, at least one Jesuit edition reached the hands of Richard Cocks before 1620.

Furthermore, in a recent essay Koakimoto has focused on a few early Sagabon and related works from the first decade of the seventeenth century. He shows that the printers of these works consciously avoided printing words that straddled two lines, even though continuous text that allows words to be split over line breaks had long been a feature of Japanese manuscripts and is still today standard procedure in printed books. Furthermore, Koakimoto finds that printers made considerable efforts to engineer each line so that no words were split between two lines: they did this by exploiting the potential of written Japanese for flexibility (for example, by replacing a Chinese graph with the same word spelled out in *hiragana*, or vice versa) and by using ligatures and other devices to alter the spacing of the text. Koakimoto's argument is that the printers must have seen some of the Jesuit Japanese imprints in which, doubtless following European practice, they endeavoured not to break words up over lines. Those who were responsible for printing the first Sagabon, he supposes, took the Jesuit editions as a model at first. This argument is not without weight, and it is difficult to explain the avoidance of words crossing the line breaks unless the printers had indeed seen some of the Japanese books printed by the Jesuits. However, since most Sagabon do not exhibit this feature, it must be supposed that the printers soon reverted to normal Japanese practice.[64]

Typography clearly flourished in early seventeenth-century Japan. It was not only sponsored by powerful individuals and institutions, it was also taken up by commercial publishers, who first made their appearance at that time. This is not to say that typography supplanted xylography as a printing technology, for some books were indeed printed xylographically during those decades. Nevertheless, typography was indubitably dominant during that period. This was not to last, however, so let us now turn instead to the subsequent decline of typography in Japan.[65]

---

[64] Koakimoto (2021). [65] This is obvious from the entries in Oka et al. (2011).

4 The Decline of Typography in Japan

In spite of the initial domination of typography in the first couple of decades of the seventeenth century, xylography gained the upper hand and went on to dominate commercial and non-commercial book production in Japan right up to the end of the nineteenth century. To put it another way, typography went into a rapid decline from which it never recovered until the Meiji period (1868–1912). Why this happened is a question that calls out for an answer. Surprisingly, this issue has gathered much less interest in Japan than the vexed question of how much early Japanese typography owed to the Korean tradition and how much to the European tradition.[66]

Before we consider why this shift took place, it is important to get some sense of the dynamics involved. In other words, when exactly did the switch take place? Using the best bibliographic information available on extant typographic and xylographic books printed in Japan between 1600 and 1650, we can get a more precise idea of the momentum. For this purpose, I have used *Edo jidai shoki shuppan nenpyō* (*Chronology of publishing in the early Edo period*), which was compiled by Oka Masahiko and his colleagues and published in 2011; it covers the period from 1592 to 1658.[67] This invaluable work lists the titles and basic bibliographic details of extant printed books year by year and identifies all the typographic books amongst them, giving locations of extant copies. However, it does have some shortcomings and these need to be acknowledged at the outset.

One shortcoming is that it does not include the contents of libraries outside Japan, except in a few rare cases, with the result that some books from that period that have not survived in Japan but have survived elsewhere are not included. This issue was partially overcome by the publication in 2019 of a supplement compiled by myself and several colleagues which covers some, but not all, of the main collections outside Japan.[68] What other shortcomings need to be acknowledged? Firstly, a considerable

---

[66] A volume published in 2009 devoted to the cultural history of typography in Japan failed to make any mention of the decline of typography in mid-seventeenth-century Japan: see Chō Shūmin (2009).

[67] Oka et al. (2011). [68] Kornicki (2019).

number of books printed in this period are undated, so they cannot be reliably placed in Oka's chronology. Secondly, since many imprints from this period survive only in one or two copies, it is certain that some imprints have not survived and are therefore missing from the lists. Thirdly, there are inevitably some mistakes: in at least one case a typographic book has not been recognised as such. Fourthly, books which were reprinted with the same dated colophon are included even though it is obvious that they must be later impressions from the original blocks, sometimes with the name of the publisher changed. Two examples will illustrate this point. There are two entries for the medical text *Igaku seiden ron* 醫學正傳論 (*On the orthodox transmission of medicine*), both bearing the date 1656, but their publishers are different, and there are three entries for the sinological study *Maoshi huowen* 毛詩或問, J. *Mōshi wakumon* (*Questions and answers on the Book of Songs*), all dated 1647 but with different publishers.[69] What must have happened in all such cases is that the original publisher sold the blocks to another publisher, who then reprinted the text without changing the date in the colophon. Since these later impressions have been included in Oka's chronology under the date of the original blocks, the numbers of xylographic titles given for each year is in some cases inflated and should therefore be reduced by perhaps five per cent. Notwithstanding these various shortcomings, for the purpose of compiling statistics in order to identify long-term trends, *Edo jidai shoki shuppan nenpyō* is indispensable, even if some small adjustments will doubtless need to be made in the future.

Using the data in *Edo jidai shoki shuppan nenpyō* and the supplement containing entries from some foreign collections, I have tabulated in Figure 3 the quantities of titles printed between 1600 and 1658 in five-year periods, distinguishing between typographic and xylographic books. The table shows that typography dominated between 1600 and 1625, but it also shows that book production increased dramatically in the years between 1625 and 1629, and that it was in that same period that xylographic books substantially exceeded the number of typographic books for the first time. Thereafter, the numbers of typographic books fell away.

[69] Oka et al. (2011), 372, 565.

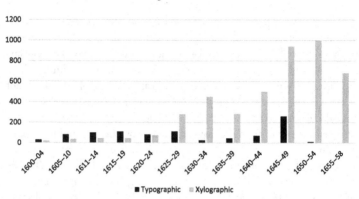

Figure 3 Typography versus xylography in Japan, 1600–58 (numbers of titles).

In the years 1644 to 1649 the number of typographic books listed in *Edo jidai shoki shuppan nenpyō* shows a dramatic jump. However, this is because each title in the Tenkaiban Buddhist canon (*Tenkaiban issaikyō* 天海版一切 経), which was printed at the Kan'eiji temple in Edo, is counted separately according to its year of publication. This edition of the Buddhist canon was printed with wooden moveable type by the monk Tenkai 天海 (1586–1643), with the support of Tokugawa Iemitsu, the third shogun, between the years 1637 and 1648.[70] As a result, the figures for the years 1644 to 1649 appear to suggest that large numbers of typographic editions were being produced, but in fact almost all of them are part of the Tenkaiban canon.[71] In the period after this (1650–4) only five typographic titles were printed, and none at all in the following five years. If the Tenkaiban Buddhist canon is excluded from consideration, then the absolute decline of typography from 1629 onwards is abundantly clear. On the other hand, the numbers of xylographic books rise a little unsteadily; the fall in the final period (1655–8) is probably in part due to

---

[70] Kawase (1967a), 1: 327, 632ff, 3: 49 (illus. 113); Mizukami (2002).

[71] The years in question are these, with the total number of typographic titles followed (in brackets) by the number of Tenkaiban titles included: 1644: 36 (32); 1645: 58 (54); 1646: 146 (131); 1647: 47 (43); 1648: 13 (11).

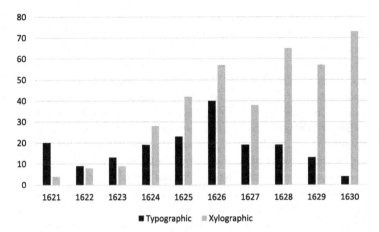

Figure 4 The numbers of typographic titles and xylographic titles printed each year between 1621 and 1630.

the fact that it includes only four years rather than five, but it is also most likely a consequence of the devastating fire in Edo in 1657. In 1658 the number of xylographic titles listed in *Edo jidai shoki shuppan nenpyō* is, at 119, at its lowest level since 1644.

What emerges from Figure 3 is that the critical decade was the 1620s. In Figure 4, therefore, I have tabulated the data year by year for the period from 1621 to 1630, in order to reveal the shift in greater detail. From this it is evident that the numbers of xylographic books exceeded typographic for the first time in 1624 and never lost the advantage after that, while typographic books rose in number of titles until 1626 and then fell off permanently after that (apart from the spike in the late 1640s when the Tenkaiban Buddhist canon was being printed).

There is no getting away from the fact that by the 1640s typography was being abandoned and commercial publishers had switched permanently back to xylography. Although it may be tempting to see this as a technological step backwards, there must have been good reasons for the reversion to xylography, and one of the aims of this Element is to look at this problem from a new angle.

It must be acknowledged, however, that this was not the absolute death of typography in Japan. There were a relatively small number of typographic books produced in the remainder of the Edo period, but they are generally known in Japanese as 'early-modern typographic editions' (*kinsei mokkatsujiban* 近世木活字版), while the typographic books printed in Japan between 1590 and 1653 are known in Japanese as 'old typographic editions' (*kokatsujiban* 古活字版). This is not really a satisfactory distinction, but it is nevertheless true that between 1653 and 1700 fewer than five typographic titles can be identified, printed in 1664, 1689 and 1693, so there was an undeniable break in continuity.[72] In the early eighteenth century there was a gentle revival of typography, and in the booksellers' catalogue of 1729 there is even, in the part devoted to Zen books, a section titled 'list of typographic editions' which gives the titles of thirty-eight Zen books, consisting of the writings and sayings of Zen prelates and teachers.[73] At the end of the eighteenth century, the transmission to Japan in 1779 of a contemporary Chinese manual of typography seems to have stimulated renewed interest, and a considerable quantity of typographic editions were produced in Japan from that time up to the Meiji Restoration in 1868, mainly by the Bakufu government, by official academies, by private academies and, in a few cases, by commercial publishers. In most cases they were printed in very limited quantities and were for restricted distribution rather than for commercial sale.[74]

Although the terminological distinction between *kokatsujiban* and *kinsei mokkatsujiban* is unconvincing, there does, nevertheless, seem to be a significant hiatus between 1653 and 1700. The point raised at the beginning of this Element still stands, therefore: we are surely in need of a good explanation for the decision of commercial publishers to abandon

---

[72] Kishimoto (1985), 64–72, and Kishimoto (1986), 76.

[73] Shidō Bunko (1962–4), 3: 105. A note at the start of this section in the catalogue of 1729 refers to Bi Sheng as the originator of typography and claims that typography was in use in Japan in 'ancient times'.

[74] Kishimoto (1986), 79. For a catalogue of 'early-modern typographic editions' (*kinsei mokkatsujiban*), see Tajihi and Nakano (1990). Often the quantity of copies printed is specified on the title page of the book in question.

typography in the early seventeenth century and for the changing balance of publications from 1626 onwards.

Commercial publishers had clearly had enough of typography, and the same was true of the non-commercial publishers such as Buddhist temples that had earlier taken to typography with enthusiasm. As I have shown already, there were very few typographic editions of any kind in the second half of the seventeenth century, and in the eighteenth century the 'early-modern typographic editions' that were produced in small numbers were quantitatively dwarfed by the xylographic editions produced by what had now become a commercial publishing industry. The best measure of the vitality of the commercial xylographic publishing industry is the catalogues of books in print published from the 1660s onwards by Kyoto booksellers. These list a wide-ranging assortment of titles, including Buddhist sutras and treatises, Chinese canonical, medical, historical, literary and other texts, and Japanese texts ranging from the classic literary works of the Heian period to new fictional literature written to be printed, as well as books on topics from board games to food preparation. For example, the catalogue of 1670 lists a total of 3,862 titles categorised as follows.[75]

Buddhist books in Chinese (various schools of Buddhism): 1,572
Buddhist books in Japanese: 116
Confucian texts in Chinese: 359
Literary writings in Chinese and dictionaries: 253
Shinto books: 79
Calendars and books of divination: 54
Military books: 132
Medical books: 247
Books of moral education in Japanese: 88
Japanese poetry and prose: 374
Books for women: 19
Noh texts for chanting: 30
Mathematical books: 18

---

[75] Moretti (2012), 269–72 (I have collapsed some of the categories); Shidō Bunko (1962–4), vol. 1.

Books on board games: 12
Books on the tea ceremony and flower arrangement: 7
Books on etiquette and food preparation: 11
Books on famous places and on art: 50
Japanese current prose and verse: 224
Primers: 85
Other, including maps, charts, scrolls and pictures: 132

What is striking about the list is, firstly, the predominance of Buddhist books, which amount to more than a third of the total, and, secondly, the fact that publishing in Japanese has developed to the point that niche markets could be catered for. Two of these niche markets were books on mathematics (*wasan* 和算) and those about board games (Go and Shōgi): books of this sort, which relied on the presentation of visual material (mathematical formulae and calculations, and the state of play in board games), depended upon the possibilities afforded by xylography.

The overall quantity of titles and the variety of books printed by 1670 show us that in the course of the first seventy years of the Edo period the supply of printed books had increased at a rapid pace. There was now indubitably a substantial market for books. They could be purchased or borrowed from bookshops in various parts of Japan, not only in the so-called 'Three Capitals' of Kyoto, Osaka and Edo. These books undoubtedly made public much information and many texts that had earlier been highly restricted in their circulation, and it is for that reason that Mary Elizabeth Berry has used the term 'library of public information' to categorise the world of commercially printed books in the Edo period.[76] A great deal of information was indeed now in the public domain in the form of accessible printed books. Nevertheless, we need to remember that the output of commercial publishers was complemented by manuscript production, and that explains why so few books on the tea ceremony, flower arrangement, etiquette and food preparation are listed in the catalogue. There remained some areas of knowledge that were not for the public and consequently were circulated in the form of manuscripts.

[76] Berry (2006).

5 Explaining the Decline of Typography

From the perspective of alphabetic societies, the most obvious reason for the abandonment of typography in seventeenth-century Japan must surely be the sheer quantity of different pieces of type needed to print texts with Chinese graphs.[77] The quantity is formidable indeed, 5000 graphs probably being the minimum in pre-modern East Asia. If, on top of that, you need a fount of small type to print the commentaries customary in the case of canonical Chinese texts, then the total required will be double. This seems to present a formidable difficulty.

Yet this is an argument that is rarely made in Japan. There are probably two reasons for that. Firstly, once the type had been made it could of course be constantly reused, so the initial effort and the investment of time and resources may indeed have been substantial by comparison with woodblock printing, but subsequent use was potentially less demanding in terms of time and resources by comparison with the constant need to have new woodblocks carved to print new books. Although pieces of wooden type were subject to the same limitation as woodblocks – namely, that they wear down with usage – nevertheless they did make it possible to print many different books using the same fount of type. Secondly, the quantity of pieces of type needed was clearly not a disincentive either in the Tangut empire, where type was prepared both for the Chinese script and for the Tangut script, or in Korea, where, in addition to Chinese graphs, type was also prepared for printing the Korean han'gŭl alphabet in several hundred syllabic blocks. Nor was it a disincentive to those individuals and institutions in Japan who used wooden moveable type for typographic printing after 1700. In the early Meiji period, too, it proved perfectly possible to use wooden moveable type for newspapers and then to develop a publishing industry based on metal type, in spite of the quantities of type needed to print with Chinese graphs. Thus, there are no signs that the quantity of type required was a significant factor affecting the practice of typography in Japan. What we

---

[77] Robinson (1993), 231, gives the number of characters as the reason that 'the invention was not widely adopted'.

need, then, is an explanation that is more specific to the circumstances of seventeenth-century Japan.

One such explanation has been offered by David Chibbett, who drew attention to the difficulties imposed by typography but not by xylography in an East Asian context: 'If more than one work was required at the same time, more type had to be manufactured, a costly and time-consuming process in an age where there was no mechanized means of manufacturing type. ... It is hard to believe, but true, that moveable type was a victim of its own success.'[78] Chibbett's argument would be more persuasive if metal type had been the norm in Japan, but in fact most commercial publishers used wooden type, which was carved by hand. Nevertheless, he is right to draw attention to the question of quantities of type, for these quantities were dictated not so much by the writing system itself as by the need to have a sufficient supply on hand to be able to keep several books in print at the same time. As Matthi Forrer has emphasised, in the inchoate publishing market of the early seventeenth century this was a serious problem: 'As soon as any publisher had a fair number of books in print, the always unpredictable demand for reprintings – with an ever growing readership – would force him to let a number of books stand in type for at least some period.'[79] Kawase Kazuma, the doyen of historians of Japanese typography, offers a more elaborate and detailed version of this argument.[80] He points out that printers were faced with an awkward choice: either to keep the forms full of type and set up to print in response to demand, thus rendering it difficult to print other works unless the printer owned huge quantities of type, or to print sufficient copies in advance to satisfy anticipated sales and store them, breaking up the type to print another work. If printers did break up the type to print other works, they then ran the risk of being embarrassed by an unexpectedly high level of demand and forced to reset the type to print more copies. That this happened all too often is in fact clear from the large number of so-called *ishokujiban* 異植字版 (differently typeset editions) of one and the same work

---

[78] Chibbett (1977), 78. [79] Forrer (1985), 62. [80] Kawase (1967a), 2: 627–30.

printed by the same printer, starting with the various editions of the *Tales of Ise* printed at Saga in Kyoto in the early years of the seventeenth century.[81] These editions appear to be identical, but close examination of the text reveals that the type has been reset: no piece of wooden type is absolutely identical to another piece bearing the same letter or graph, so visual comparison reveals the differences.

It is easy to appreciate the inconvenience of having to reset type frequently in order to print further copies, particularly when a comparison is made with woodblocks, which could be stored and easily reused in response to demand. The arguments outlined here, then, are based on an understanding of the nature of the market in seventeenth-century Japan, when books would remain in print for decades, and on an estimation of the economics of publishing, for sluggish sales would mean that recouping the capital investment would be a slow process. At this time, in the early seventeenth century, commercial publishers were still in their infancy, but demand was growing and the reading public was changing rapidly. In this context, it is argued, xylography was better placed than typography to respond to the market. This has now become the standard argument, and it has been restated by Nakane Katsu, who cannot, however, put his finger on a causal connection between the changes in the market and the technological shift from typography to xylography.[82] Yet, as we will see in due course, there does exist concrete evidence that can put some flesh on this argument.

Before we examine the nature of that concrete evidence, however, we must acknowledge that there are some other possible explanations for the abandonment of typography. The most original argument is that of Ōuchida Sadao, who is unconvinced that the market was changing so fast in the early seventeenth century as to necessitate abandoning moveable type.[83] His radically new proposal is to connect the abandonment of typography with the suppression of Christianity that was certainly being carried out at the same time. His suggestion – that typography might have been mistakenly

---

[81] See, for example, the textually identical copies of *Enju satsuyō* printed apparently in the same year (1599), with different or rearranged type: Oka et al. (2011), 10–11.

[82] Nakane (1999), 151.   [83] Ōuchida (2000), 23–39.

associated with the proscribed and dangerous religion and avoided for reasons of safety – is attractive and plausible at first sight, but it does in fact contain inherent weaknesses. The first is that both the court and the shogunal household had engaged in typographic printing even when Christianity was coming under pressure, so it is difficult to suppose that it was seen as a suspect technology. The second is that the abandonment of typography was very gradual rather than sudden as the persecutions of missionaries and Christian believers became more severe. It is certainly true that the Shimabara Rebellion of 1637–8, in which many Christians took part, occurred at about the same time that commercial printers were abandoning typography, but post hoc is not necessarily propter hoc. Furthermore, as we have already seen, it was in the 1620s that the shift took place, not the late 1630s. And, finally, it is difficult to believe that the third shogun, Tokugawa Iemitsu, would have sponsored the publication of the Tenkaiban Buddhist Canon in the 1640s if typography had been seen as a suspect technology.

Other arguments can be dealt with more briefly. Nakano bases his explanation not so much on the problems of moveable type as on the superiority of woodblocks as a form of capital investment.[84] It is certainly true that woodblocks had a potential life of 200 years and could be sold and resold: for example, in 1673 blocks were carved to print *Nihon sandai jitsuroku* 日本三代実録 (*True records of three Japanese reigns*), a chronicle which was completed in 901 and was the last of the Six National Histories. Those same woodblocks were still being used to print copies in 1864, albeit in the hands of a different publisher.[85] It is certainly true, then, that printing blocks potentially had a very long life and that the capital investment in them could be recouped, either by selling them on to another publisher or by using a plane to remove the text and reuse the blocks for a new work. However, it is far from clear that printers would have appreciated these advantages in the early seventeenth century, or that this would have been a factor in their choice of printing technology.

Finally, although aesthetic factors have not featured in arguments hitherto, it is worth drawing attention to the fact that while typography

[84] Nakano (1995), 31, 34–5. [85] Hayashi and Kornicki (1991), 218, #1169.

was eminently suitable for Chinese works, which were usually printed in the regular *kaisho* style (square graphs), it was more difficult to reproduce the flow of Japanese calligraphy in moveable type. Nevertheless, valiant efforts were made through the use of ligatures in the *hiragana* syllabary in an attempt to Japanise typography. Such typographic ligatures can be seen in the so-called Sagabon printed in Kyoto by Suminokura Soan and in the *Guide to prolonging life* (*Enju satsuyō*) (see Figure 1).[86] Conversely, Japanese books printed with wooden moveable type in the eighteenth and nineteenth centuries are identifiable immediately on account of the spaces that necessarily occur between each piece of type. This is because those texts were usually printed in a mixture of Chinese graphs and the square *katakana* syllabary (Figure 5). A further consideration is the inclusion of illustrations in printed books. There was not in principle any difficulty in including them in typographic books, although they were necessarily printed with wooden blocks. Many early typographic books in fact included xylographic illustrations. It may well have been easier to print text and illustrations together using the same woodblocks, but the desire to include illustrations does not on its own provide a convincing reason for abandoning typography. Nevertheless, we should recognise that xylographic editions of Japanese (as opposed to Chinese) texts throughout the Edo period were characterised by profuse illustrations and calligraphic variety. Wooden moveable type could not reproduce that calligraphic variety, for all the books printed using the same fount of type inevitably shared the same calligraphic appearance.

Since there is no available documentary evidence providing the seventeenth-century printer's point of view, these various explanations have been generated in modern times ex post facto. As a result, they are all somewhat speculative, albeit in some cases attractive, and they are all at some remove from the concrete evidence provided by seventeenth-century books themselves. They also have the shortcoming that they are largely generic and not specific to the circumstances of early seventeenth-century Japan. I shall now turn, therefore, to the very particular evidence provided by two early Japanese medical texts.

[86] For the Sagabon, see the illustrations in Kinoshita (2000), 56–73.

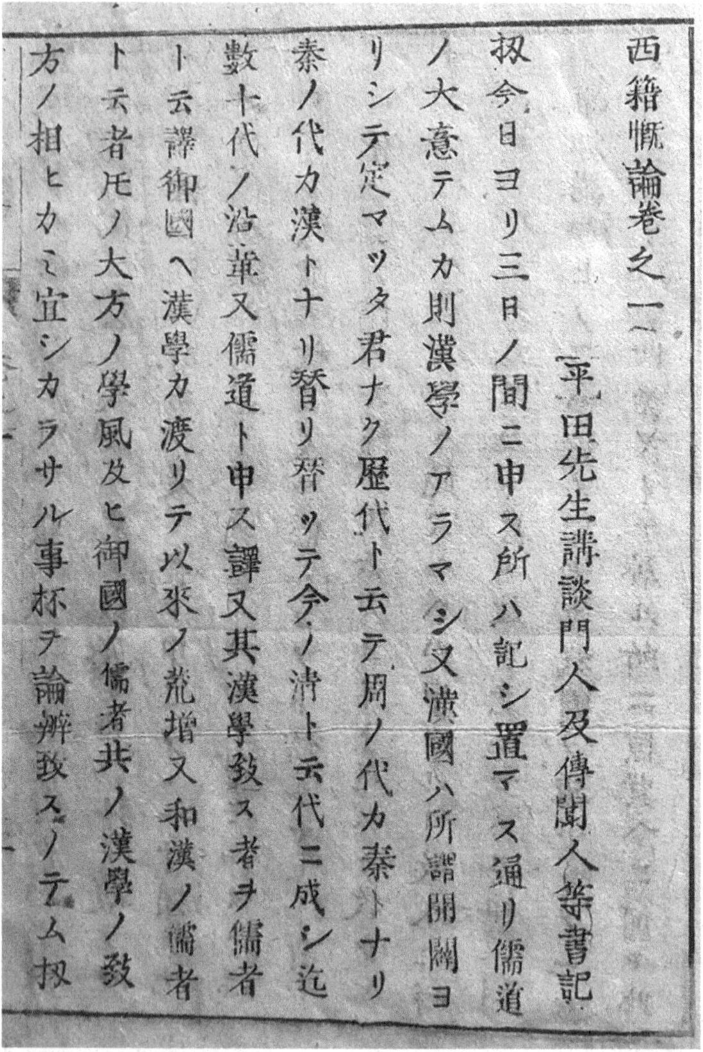

西籍慨論巻之一　　平田先生講談門人及傳聞人等書記

抑今日ヨリ三日ノ間ニ申ス所ハ記シ置マス通リ儒道
ノ大意テムカ則漢學ノアラマシ又漢國ハ所謂開闢ヨ
リシテ定マツタ君ナク歴代ト云テ周ノ代カ秦トナリ
秦ノ代カ漢トナリ替リ替ツテ今ノ清ト云代ニ成シ迄
數十代ノ沿革又儒道ト申ス譯又其漢學致ス者ヲ儒者
ト云譯御國ヘ漢學カ渡リテ以来ノ荒増又和漢ノ儒者
ト云者斤ノ大方ノ學風及ヒ御國ノ儒者共ノ漢學ノ致
方ノ相ヒカミ宜シカラサル事杯ヲ論辨致スノテム抑

Figure 5 The opening page of Hirata Atsutane's *Seiseki gairon* (*General account of western books*), which was a critique of Confucianism. It was printed in 1858 in a limited edition of 100 copies. The text is in a mixture of *katakana* and Chinese chateracters. Author's collection.

6 Two Early Seventeenth-Century Medical Texts

The significance of the two medical texts to be examined in this section lies in the fact that they were both printed in the early seventeenth century, first in typographic editions and then in xylographic editions, in quick succession. They therefore allow us to get much closer to the choices that were being made by printers who were shifting from typography to xylography at the time in question.

The earlier of the two books is *Saiminki* 済民記 (*A record to assist the people*), which was probably drafted by Manase Dōsan 曲直瀬道三 (1507–94), a figure who is widely considered to have begun the process of the Japanisation and vernacularisation of medicine in Japan. Printed copies of *Saiminki*, which was first published long after the death of Dōsan, lack any indication of authorship, but the text has often been attributed to Manase Gensaku (1549–1631), the adopted son and heir of Dōsan. However, recent research has cast doubt on the role of Gensaku as author in this and other similar cases, and the accepted view is rather that Gensaku merely revised and supplemented works that had earlier been written by Dōsan.[87] This is not an insignificant point: it was during his period of exile in Hitachi (now Ibaraki Prefecture) that Gensaku turned his attention to the provision of medical information for the common people, and *Saiminki* is a work that well accords with this shift in focus, for it contains advice on how to treat various ailments using medicaments that were readily available in Japan.[88]

The second work is *Shoshitsu kinkōshū* 諸疾禁好集 (*Collection of things that are good and bad for all diseases*; hereafter referred to as *Shoshitsu*), which was written and published by a man called Baiju in 1626. Baiju was a doctor, but was also much engaged in publishing in the early seventeenth century. It turns out, in fact, that quite a number of the earliest publishers of the time were of medical background, and they did not restrict themselves

---

[87] Endō and Nakamura (2004), 547–68. On p. 553 the authors suggest that the title *Saiminki* may, in addition to its surface meaning, carry additional references to two of the Chinese medical works upon which it is based.

[88] This vernacularisation of medicine and pharmaceuticals was new in Japan but was already well established in Korea: Suh (2020).

to publishing medical works. Like *Saiminki*, *Shoshitsu* was printed in a small horizontal format, which was unusual at the time, and which has a bearing on the reasons for the technological shift.

Although I shall be focusing on these two works, *Saiminki* and *Shoshitsu*, it is important to appreciate at the outset that they belong to a very popular genre of medical primers in horizontal format that began to be produced in the late sixteenth century and continued to be popular until the early eighteenth century, although they have attracted very little scholarly attention so far. All of these works rely upon Chinese pharmaceutical knowledge and dietary medicine that had begun to reach Japan in the Heian period (794–1185), if not before, as is apparent from the quotations in *Ishinpō* 医心方 (*Prescriptions from the heart of medicine*), a compendium of continental medicine compiled in Japan in the late tenth century. *Shoshitsu*, for example, explicitly draws upon recently imported knowledge in the form of two late Ming medical manuals. One of them is *Baochi quanshu* 保赤全書 (*The complete book of protecting children*), which had appeared in a Japanese typographic edition published by Baiju himself just two years earlier in 1624.[89] The other is *Da sheng lu* 達生録 (*Account of attaining life*): since the only known Japanese edition of *Da sheng lu* is that of 1649, well after the publication of *Shoshitsu*, Baiju must have relied upon an imported Chinese edition. Many of these Chinese medical manuals were organised with separate sections on each medicinal plant rather than on specific medical conditions, and in each section the author explains the medical benefits of one plant. On the other hand, *Saiminki* and *Shoshitsu* are both focused on medical conditions and on the plants and foodstuffs that can ameliorate or aggravate them, so they are both of a practical rather than scientific character.

Of the two works under consideration, *Shoshitsu* has survived in far few copies and appears to have had a shorter commercial life (Table 1).

Almost all copies bear a date equivalent to 1626, but the first edition was clearly the typographic edition, for the xylographic editions have a small amount of new material added on the last page. *Saiminki*, on the other hand,

---

[89] This Japanese typographic edition of *Baochi quanshu* includes the original prefaces, of which the most recent is dated 1601. The only known copy is in the National Archives of Japan (Kokuritsu Kōbunshokan, 303–288).

Table 1 Extant copies of *Shoshitsu kinkōshū*

Date	Type	Locations	Notes
1626	typographic	Ken'ikai Toshokan, Tōkyō	
1626	xylographic	Wellcome Trust, London; Kyōu Shooku, Osaka (杏 2312); Tōkyō Kasei Gakuin Daigaku Ōe Bunko; Tsurumi University, Yokohama; Miyagi-ken Toshokan, Sendai; Tōkyō Rika Daigaku; Naitō Kinen Kusuri Hakubutsukan	
1626	xylographic	Kyōu Shooku, Osaka (杏2311)	Retains the original colophon but bound at the front is a single sheet with the name of the Kyoto publisher, Tsurugaya Kyūhei, and the blocks are somewhat worn. A later reprint.
	xylographic	Kyūshū University. 490/ シ −4/1	An undated later reprint from the original wood blocks.

survives in more copies representing more editions: there was still a demand for it in 1658, when the last known edition was printed (Table 2).

What is it that unites these two books and justifies treating them in tandem here? Firstly, there is the fact that they both appeared initially in typographic editions and subsequently in xylographic editions. In the case of *Shoshitsu*, the two editions bear the same date, so the xylographic edition most likely appeared very soon after the typographic edition. *Saiminki*, on the other hand, is a little harder to pin down. There was a typographic edition in 1617 and a xylographic edition in 1631, but there was also an undated typographic and an undated xylographic edition, which were almost certainly printed between those two dates.

The second, and more important, point in common between these two books is that the shift was not merely a matter of printing technology. This is because the xylographic editions all take advantage of the greater flexibility of xylography to add glosses and non-textual features to the text. The typographic editions mostly lack these glosses, so readers added their own by hand, as the extant copies show.

The glosses are of key importance here, so some elaboration is needed. The glosses are of two kinds: one consists of pronunciation glosses (*furigana*) printed in a smaller size to the right of Chinese graphs, which give the desired Japanese pronunciation of the graphs in question, and the other consists of syntactical glosses (*kunten* 訓点) attached to texts in literary Chinese, which enable readers to construe the Chinese text as if it were Japanese – in other words, to translate it mentally (or aloud) into Japanese.[90] These glosses raise several questions: why were the printed glosses necessary, and was it not possible to supply them in typographic editions?

The syntactical glosses (*kunten*) were necessary because few Japanese sinologists, let alone general readers, had the ability to read unmediated texts in literary Chinese. In this respect, Japanese intellectuals differed from their counterparts in Korea and Vietnam, where the official examination systems placed a premium on the ability to read and write Chinese without vernacular assistance. There was no such examination system in Japan and as a result it was a rare scholar indeed who could parse a raw text in literary Chinese. Even

---

[90] On *kundoku*, see Lurie (2011) and Kornicki (2018).

Table 2 Extant copies of *Saiminki*

Date	Type	Locations	Notes
1617	typographic	Kyōu Shooku, Osaka; Kyoto University	All editions except that of 1658 are printed in a mixture of Chinese graphs and *katakana*.
Undated	typographic	Tōyō Bunko, Tokyo 三-AJ-7	There used to be a copy in the Yasuda Bunko, but this was destroyed in an air raid in 1945: Kawase (1967a) 1: 336.
Undated	xylographic	Tōyō Bunko XV-4-15; Ken'ikai Toshokan, Tōkyō (2 copies)	Not printed from the same woodblocks as the 1643 or 1647 editions.
1631	xylographic	International Research Center for Japanese Studies, Kyoto; Jingū Bunko; Tamagawa University.	Published by Sugita Ryōan.
1643	xylographic	Unknown	Published by Ōwada Ikan. Image in Gotō (2003), 452.
1647	xylographic	Okayama University; Kansai University; Kyushū University; Kokubungaku Kenkyū Shiryōkan, Tōkyō; author's collection.	No publisher given. Not printed from the same woodblocks as the 1643 edition.

Table 2 (Cont.)

Date	Type	Locations	Notes
1651	xylographic	Meirindō Bunko, Chōritsu Takanabe Toshokan, Miyazaki Prefecture.	No publisher given. Not printed from the same woodblocks as the 1647 edition.
1651	xylographic	Chiba University	Published by Nakano Tarōzaemon.
1658	xylographic	National Diet Library; Ken'ikai Toshokan, Tōkyō	Published by Murakami Kanbei of Kyoto in a mixture of graphs and *hiragana*. The Ken'ikai Toshokan copy lacks the last two folios and hence the colophon. No other *hiragana* editions are known.

Hayashi Razan 林羅山 (1583–1657), one of the best sinologists in early seventeenth-century Japan, routinely wrote glosses in the raw Chinese texts he read, thus keeping a record of how he construed each text. Because publishers recognised that readers needed the crutches provided by syntactical glosses, throughout the Edo period they included abundant syntactical glosses in the Chinese texts they printed. This was, of course, for sound commercial reasons: texts thus equipped with glosses were far more accessible and could therefore reach a larger market than texts without glosses.

The *furigana* glosses, on the other hand, were necessary in the first place because they, too, enabled publishers to reach much larger markets, including people with an unsteady command of Chinese graphs. Chinese graphs had long been embedded in the Japanese writing system, but their Japanese articulations were not fixed, so the glosses showed readers how the authors wanted the graphs to be read in Japanese. Once typography was abandoned and xylography reigned unchallenged, the provision of extensive pronunciation glosses became standard, and that applied even to newspapers in the early Meiji period.

At first sight, it may seem surprising that *furigana* glosses were rarely printed before the Edo period: after all, xylography made the inclusion of glosses a simple matter. However, most books printed before the Edo period were aimed at a limited market of learned monks, so there was no need to make allowances for readers with a lower level of literacy. There were, certainly, a few exceptions, such as the 1372 and 1387 editions of the Lotus sutra (*Myōhō rengekyō* 妙法蓮華経), and the 1386 edition of a glossed edition of the Lotus sutra (*Hokkekyō onkun* 法華経音訓), which were instead intended for less sophisticated lay Buddhists. In several sixteenth-century editions of the dictionary *Setsuyōshū* 節用集 each word is equipped with *furigana* glosses in *katakana* to indicate how it should be pronounced. Similarly, *Shūbun inryaku* 聚分韻略, a popular handbook for writing Chinese poetry compiled in 1306 by a Japanese monk, was also printed at some time in the sixteenth century with *furigana* glosses in *katakana*. In all other cases, however, readers had to write in their own glosses by hand, as many extant copies show.[91] It is surely

---

[91] Kawase (1970), 1: 231, 280–5, 442–3, 447, 2: plates 273, 537–9; *Hokkekyō onkun* (1931); Kuboo (2008); Yamada (1984).

significant that many of these books were either practical in nature and designed to be reference books, or were aimed at a market of Buddhist believers who were unable to read the Chinese translations of Buddhist scriptures; it is doubtless for this reason that these were the first books to be printed in Japan with the *furigana* glosses that made them more useful and accessible for users. At any rate, it is important to note that printed *furigana* glosses were a new feature of Japanese books that appeared in just three books printed in the fourteenth century and a few more in the sixteenth century. Such glosses were also included in some of the typographic editions published by the Jesuits, such as the dictionary *Rakuyōshū* 落葉集 (1598) and *Contemptus Mundi* (1610).[92]

Japanese typographic publishers in the early seventeenth century were well aware of the benefits of glosses, and consequently some of them made elaborate attempts to include *furigana* glosses and/or syntactic glosses in their typographic editions. Two methods were tried out: one was to use smaller founts of type in separate rows to the right of the graphs being glossed (Figure 6), and the other was to carve (since most Japanese typography used wooden type) special pieces of type with the *furigana* glosses included with the graphs (Figure 7). Since some Chinese graphs were pronounced in very different ways according to context, the second method necessitated preparing several versions of the same graph, each with a different *furigana* gloss. For example, the graph 無 indicates negation or absence, but it can either appear in compound words such as *mujirushi* 無印 (meaning 'unbranded', familiar now in the contracted name of the chain store Muji, known in Japan as Mujirushi), in which it is pronounced mu, or in Japanese negated forms such as *nakereba* 無け れ ば ('since/if there is not'), in which it is pronounced na. Consequently, a printer would have to prepare two sets of type with this graph: one with the gloss mu and the other with the gloss na. It will be obvious that both these methods of providing glosses required the printer to invest more money in type production.

[92] Illustrations of both texts are included in Sasaki (2022), 52, 55. See also https://digital-archives.sophia.ac.jp/laures-kirishitan-bunko/.

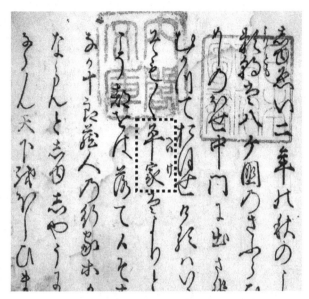

Figure 6 *Karaito sōshi*, undated typographic edition in the National Archives of Japan. There are frequent interlineal glosses. The word with a dotted outline in the middle is the word Heike, the name of one of the leading families in ancient Japan, and beside it to the right is a gloss giving the pronunciation in hiragana script.

The question of glosses naturally had an impact upon the publishers of the typographic first editions of *Shoshitsu* and *Saiminki*. Although they both drew on the Chinese pharmacopoeia, they were intended for a popular market and consequently faced particular difficulties: a plethora of rare or obscure Chinese graphs which none but medical specialists could be expected to know. The two publishers responded differently.

The unnamed publisher of the typographic 1617 edition of *Saiminki* left readers to fend for themselves. Consequently, readers had to work their

Figure 7 The opening section of the 1627 typographic edition of the Japanese translation of the Ming-dynasty political manual *Dijian tushuo* (J. *Teikan zusetsu*) showing the text printed with wooden type that incorporated pronunciation glosses on the right. National Diet Library, Tōkyō.

way through the text on their own and struggle with the unfamiliar vocabulary. In the copy preserved in Kyoto University Library a reader wrote the *furigana* glosses by hand in the text. Nevertheless, it is clear that the publisher of this edition was aware of the restrictions imposed by typography, for he cut special type with white graphs on a black background to head the sections listing the 'recommended' and 'forbidden' foodstuffs for each ailment. Such white-on-black graphs and various non-script decorative devices were easy to produce in a xylographic imprint, which simply reproduced whatever could be written or drawn on paper, while typographic imprints required extra pieces of type (Figure 8). By contrast, the undated xylographic edition of *Saiminki* (Figure 9), which is closely based on the typographic edition, takes full advantage of the possibilities afforded by xylography to provide *furigana* glosses for every graph, including the heading denoting 'forbidden', as well as punctuation separating the items in the list of 'forbidden' foodstuffs. At the bottom of the fifth line from the right, the last graph is furnished with two alternative readings, one on each side.

Baiju, however, went further for his typographic edition of *Shoshitsu*. Although he was already an experienced publisher of typographic editions, for this book he went the extra mile and prepared some type with attached *furigana* glosses for the first time. As can be seen from Figure 10, he only did this to a limited extent, with the result that many graphs lack glosses; they have instead been equipped with glosses by hand by a reader who entered the *furigana* while reading the text.[93] In his typographic edition of *Shoshitsu* Baiju was clearly pushing at the frontiers of typography, endeavouring to provide some glosses to make the text more accessible to readers without medical expertise. He did the same in 1624 in his typographic edition of *Baochi quanshu* (*The complete book of protecting children*), at the end of which he provides a numbered list of medicines cross-referenced in the text. For the convenience of readers, the numbers were printed with white text on black background so that they stood out more clearly.[94]

---

[93] On the typographic edition, see Kornicki (2015).

[94] *Baochi quanshu*, National Archives of Japan (Kokuritsu Kōbunshokan, 303–288), vol. 2, ff. 12°–86°.

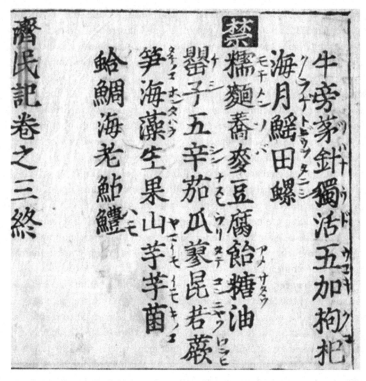

Figure 8 The end of the 1617 typographic edition of *Saiminki*. Note the handwritten *furigana* glosses to the right of most graphs and the white-on-black piece of type for the graph signifying 'forbidden' at the top. Kyoto University Library.

It is my contention, therefore, that both Baiju and the anonymous publisher of *Saiminki* were exploring ways of getting around some of the limitations imposed by typography so as to make their popular medical works more accessible to potential readers. The unusual format of

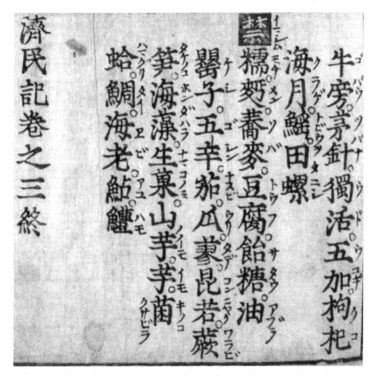

Figure 9 The end of the undated (1620s?) xylographic edition of *Saiminki*, which provides glosses for every graph. National Diet Library, Tōkyō.

these and other early medical books – small, portable and horizontal in orientation – marks them out as practical manuals aimed at a popular readership and therefore without the portentous dimensions of most books at the time.

Very soon after he had published his typographic edition of *Shoshitsu* in 1626, and very possibly later the same year, Baiju must have realised that there was an easier way of serving the same end, and that was to turn to

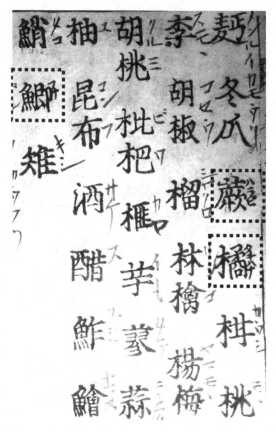

Figure 10 The 1626 typographic edition of *Shoshitsu kinkōshū*. The graphs outlined with dotted lines are those with *furigana* included in the type; all the other *furigana* were added by hand. Ken'ikai Toshokan, Tōkyō.

xylography. His xylographic edition of *Shoshitsu*, which is also dated 1626, reveals that he was fully aware of the potential of xylography as a means of making difficult texts accessible (Figure 11). On the first page alone we can identify the following features:

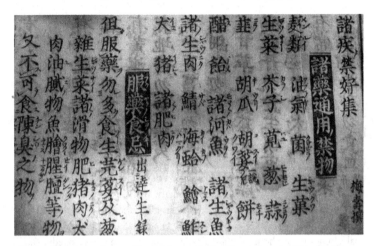

Figure 11 The xylographic edition of *Shoshitsu*, dated 1626. Wellcome Trust, London.

1. Section headings printed in white on black background. The one near the middle of the page has *furigana* glosses, also in white on black.
2. *Furigana* glosses for many words written in Chinese graphs.
3. The left half of the page consists of a quotation in literary Chinese from *Da sheng lu* and it is equipped with syntactical glosses (*kunten*) that enabled Japanese readers to construe the Chinese text and mentally translate it into Japanese.

The fact that only one copy of the typographic edition is extant while nine copies of the xylographic edition are known today is perhaps an indication that the xylographic edition was produced in greater numbers and that Baiju had made the right call.

This was not the only book that Baiju published consecutively in typographic and xylographic editions. Another example is *The fourteen bodily tracts explained* (*Shisijing fahui*, J. *Jūshikei hakki*), a study of the theory and practice of acupuncture focusing on the fourteen bodily tracts. This work was written in 1341 by the Chinese physician Hua Shou 滑壽 (1304–86),

and it was first printed in 1364 in an edition edited by Xue Kai 薛鎧 of the Ming dynasty. It was printed in Japan in 1596 and was in fact one of the first books to be printed with moveable type in Japan. Baiju, too, printed a typographic edition in 1618, but in 1631 he published a xylographic edition that was a facsimile of the Ming edition.[95]

In short, typography was no match for xylography when it came to including extensive *furigana* pronunciation glosses or syntactical glosses to printed texts. Quite a few publishers pushed the possibilities of typography to the limit, accepting the additional costs involved in having extra type carved. Many examples of typographic experimentation of this kind can be given. To give three cases, the 1609 edition of the botanical textbook *Shōrui honzō jorei* 証類本草序例 included many pieces of type showing the graphs in white against a black background; the 1617 edition of the Buddhist treatise *Jūjūshin kōmyōmoku* 十住心論広名目 includes syntactical glosses throughout; and an edition of the Chinese encyclopedia *Gujin shiwen leiju* 古今事文類聚 (J. *Kokon jibun ruiju*), dating from around 1620, includes various devices to divide up the sections, including graphs enclosed in boxes.[96]

Like all the other publishers of typographic editions, Baiju left no financial records, memoirs or even any correspondence. Very little is known about him, apart from the books that he published.[97] He began publishing in 1608 when he issued an edition of a study of *The yellow emperor's classic of internal medicine* (*Huangdi neijing suwen zhuzheng fawei* 黃帝内經素問註證發微, J. *Kōtei naikei somon chūshō hatsubi*), a substantial work written by Ma Shi 馬蒔 in the early sixteenth century. He must at this point have acquired a fount of type, given that he published at least one work typographically every year for a number of years; whether he purchased the fount of type ready made or had it

---

[95] The 1618 edition is preserved in Tenri Library, and the 1631 edition in the National Institute of Japanese Literature and the University of Chicago Library. They are listed in Oka et al. (2011), 72, 150.

[96] Sorimachi (1972), 66–7, 250–1, 344–5.

[97] Kawase (1967b); Tajihi (2007). It should be noted that Kawase gets the title of *Shoshitsu* wrong, giving it as *Shobyō kinkōshū* 諸病禁好集.

specially carved we do not know. Before the year 1608 was out Baiju had published another edition of exactly the same work, and he published a third edition in 1609, which suggests that he was underestimating the market for this work and having to reset the type.[98] By the time that Baiju published *Shoshitsu* in 1626, he had already been using his fount of type year after year to print Chinese texts typographically, so why did he switch to xylography? It is surely unlikely that he gave much thought to the long-term advantages of xylography (the ability to recoup capital investment by selling the blocks to another publisher or the possibility of keeping a work in print for decades). His immediate problem was, rather, how to make a work of popular medicine accessible to Japanese readers, and to that end he first experimented on a limited scale with type which was equipped with *furigana*.

As we have already seen, it was perfectly possible to accommodate the desire to include *furigana* in typography employing wooden type. Similarly, European typography in the sixteenth century could accommodate multiple typefaces as well as non-textual material. Take, for example, the two editions of the works of Galen printed in Venice by Lucantonio Giunta. The first, printed in 1541–2, has a complex title page incorporating text printed in italic, Roman and Greek, in various sizes and styles, as well as symbols, motifs and, all around the edge, woodcuts depicting the life of Galen. In the second, printed in 1551–2, we find text wrapped around woodcuts which show patients being treated in bed.[99]

Baiju could, therefore, have taken his experiment further and had a lot more type carved with glosses attached. Type equipped with *furigana* glosses could indeed have become the standard form when printing Japanese texts if typography had remained in use. But let us consider just what that would have meant in practice. Figure 12 shows the opening page of a medical reference work printed xylographically at some time in the middle of the seventeenth century. This single page contains

[98] Kawase (1967a), vol. 2, figs. 167–9.

[99] I consulted the copies in the University of Bologna, which are currently on display in the Anatomy Theatre, Bologna.

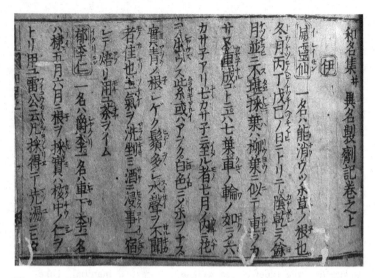

Figure 12 The first page of *Wamyōshū narabini imyō seisaiki*, a reference work providing the Japanese names and some further details of medicinal plants and other items featuring in Chinese pharmaceutical works. There were two typographic editions printed in 1623 and 1625, but this undated copy is one of the many subsequent xylographic editions. Note the extensive pronunciation glosses (*furigana*) and the double cartouches around the headings. Author's collection.

eighty-nine graphs with *furigana* glosses and thirty graphs without them. Amongst them are the graphs 月 and 用, which appear both with and without glosses, and the graph 葉, which appears twice, each time with a different gloss. The graph 聞 appears with the gloss *kika* because it is preceded by a graph indicating negation and therefore needs to be read in its negative form, but the same graph can in other contexts be read *ki(ku)*, *bun* or *mon*. A printer desiring to provide glosses for these usages would therefore need to lay in four different versions of this one graph alone.

The same applies to the graph 生, which appears here with the gloss *shō*: it is commonly also read *sei*, *ʑei* or *u(mu)*. It is clear, then, that in order to print typographically the extensive glosses that were provided in seventeenth-century xylographic publications would require a huge increase in the number of different pieces of type required – at least double the number. Technically it would be perfectly possible, but it would need a much more substantial initial investment.

What persuaded Baiju, who was already an experienced printer, to abandon typography? It was probably not the cost that deterred him, though the logistical problem of having to make and store a great deal more type may have been a consideration. Rather, his decision to reprint *Shoshitsu* xylographically was surely a recognition of the greater flexibility of xylography. He made the switch primarily in order to provide more extensive *furigana* glosses in *Shoshitsu*, and this was the path followed by all publishers by the middle of the seventeenth century, no matter what kind of texts they were printing.

What explains their abandonment of typography? In the first place, it is clear that typography was taken up in Japan with some enthusiasm at first. That may have been because Korean moveable type accompanied the many books looted from Korea, which included typographic books, and which were certainly welcomed and treasured in Japan. Or it may have been the prestige of the imperial institution that was decisive when Emperor Go-Yōzei had the *Classic of filial piety* printed in 1593. In any case, as in Korea, the adoption of typography by emperors, shoguns and well-endowed temples meant that the initial capital investment was not a problem. There was no need to balance the initial outlay against commercial returns, for none of these were commercial printing operations. What is more, they were content to print one work at a time, and the output in terms of numbers of titles was small, though we are not in a position to say how many copies were printed of each title. As mentioned earlier, the colophon of the *Preface to the profound meaning of the lotus sutra* indicates that 100 copies were printed in 1595, and this may have been typical. However, it is also clear that the Sagabon *Ise monogatari* and other works were reprinted with rearranged type on several occasions, so it cannot be assumed that typography was only used in Japan for small editions.

Since typography was subsequently taken up by some of the first commercial publishers in Japan, it is evident that they were prepared to make the initial investment required for the acquisition of a fount of type, in the expectation that they would publish numerous works using the same type so as to recoup their investment. However, as Chibbett, Kawase and Nakane have argued (see Section 5), the growth of the book market, especially from the 1620s onwards, created problems for commercial printers using typography, for they did not have sufficient quanitities of type to keep several books in print at the same time. They seem to have frequently underestimated demand and consequently to have been forced to reset the type to produce further copies of books they had already published, as mentioned earlier. In these circumstances, xylography had the edge over typography, for carved woodblocks could simply be taken out of storage to print further copies. In other words, in an expanding market for printed books the economic advantage shifted in favour of xylography, and in addition, as Kai-Wing Chow has argued, xylography offered would-be publishers the opportunity to enter the market with a modest amount of capital.[100]

It was, after all, the flexibility of xylography and the lower level of initial capital investment required that explains the reversion to xylography in early seventeenth-century Japan. That flexibility can be understood in different ways. One was the possibility of keeping works in print for a long time – sometimes more than 100 years – thus enabling publishers to have several works in print at the same time. Furthermore, the modest capital investment required to have the woodblocks carved could be partly recouped by selling the blocks to other publishers or, in the worst case, by planing the blocks down and reusing them for a different work. In the Japanese context, an important

---

[100] Chow (2004). Chow rightly rejects the Eurocentric view that xylography was in some way backward by comparison with typography. See also Chia (2000) and Fitzgerald (2024) for a discussion of the relative roles of xylography and typography in China.

part of that flexibility was the ability to respond to market demand by making texts more accessible through various forms of glossing. After all, it was only through xylography that extensive glossing could be provided easily, cheaply and routinely.

The connection between printed glosses and the development of a commercial market for books in seventeenth-century Japan can hardly be doubted. Prior to 1600 almost all books were printed without pronunciation glosses or syntactical glosses, as mentioned earlier. By contrast, printed glosses became standard and extensive in Edo-period publications, and very few books lacked them. This represents a significant change in the *mise-en-page* of both Chinese and Japanese texts printed in Japan. Chinese texts were in effect Japanised by being equipped with extensive syntactic glosses, and Japanese texts routinely included pronunciation glosses. As a result, many texts which had been printed typographically without glosses in the first three decades of the seventeenth century were later in the century reprinted xylographically with extensive added glosses.

Take, for example, Hayashi Razan's *Shigenshō* 厄言抄, which contains short extracts from Chinese philosophical and historical literature followed by lengthy explanations in Japanese using Chinese graphs and *katakana*. The postface is dated 1620 and it is likely that the typographic edition was published in that year, although this edition does not indicate a date of printing or the name of the publisher. The short extracts in the typographic edition are equipped with syntactic glosses (*kunten*), for this is a work designed to introduce readers to some significant passages written in literary Chinese, and such readers, Razan rightly supposes, lacked the ability to construe the literary Chinese without assistance. Razan's postface, however, was unglossed and there were no pronunciation glosses (*furigana*) in Razan's explanations. At some time between 1620 and 1649 (when a new dated edition appeared), the same publisher or a different one produced a xylographic edition. This was a facsimile (*kabusebori*, see Section 2) of the 1620 edition, but beforehand *furigana* were added here and there by hand to Razan's explanations and his postface was fully equipped with *kunten* (Figure 13).

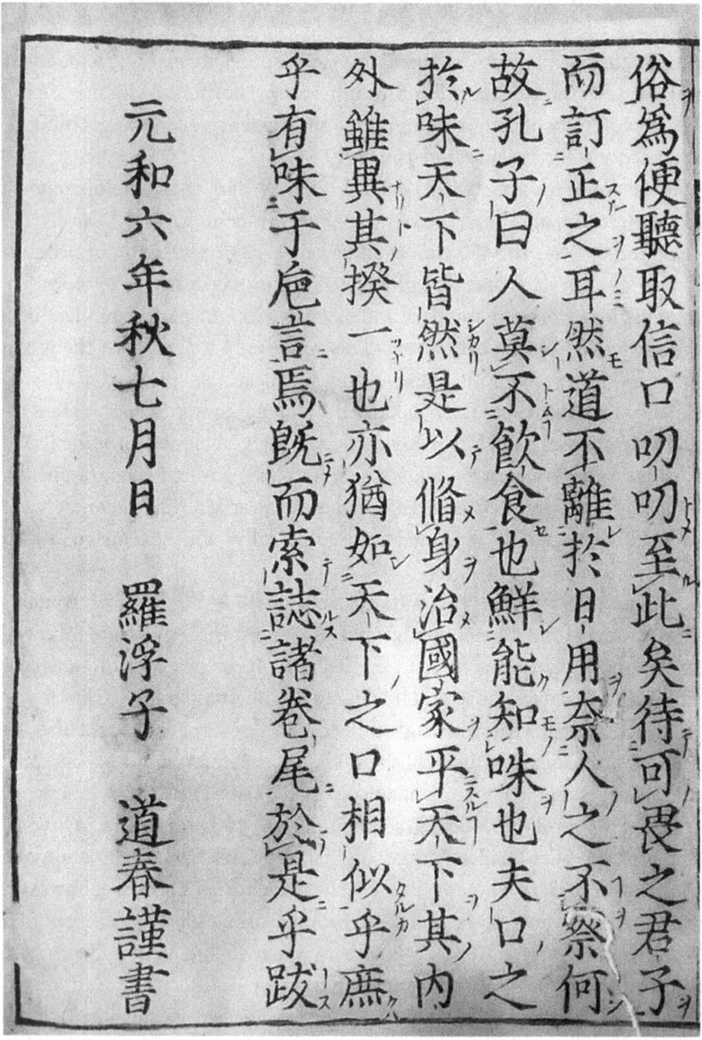

俗爲便聽取信口叨叨至此矣待可畏之君子
而訂正之耳然道不離於日用奈人之不察何
故孔子曰人莫不飲食也鮮能知味也夫口之
於味天下皆然是以偹身治國家平天下其内
外雖異其揆一也亦猶如天下之口相似乎庶
乎有味于厄言焉既而索誌諸卷尾於是乎跋

元和六年秋七月日　羅浮子　道春謹書

Figure 13 The postface, dated 1620, of the xylographic edition of Hayashi Razan's *Shigenshō*, printed at some time between 1620 and 1649. Author's collection.

Xylography was a rational choice because it offered the possibility of making texts more accessible, which for commercial publishers was an important consideration. In the case of the two medical books described earlier, it made imported Chinese medical knowledge accessible in the vernacular. And, in general, canonical Chinese texts, such as the *Analects* of Confucius, could now be made available with extensive syntactical glosses that made them accessible to the mass of would-be readers who could not cope with unmediated Chinese but, with the aid of the glosses, could translate the text into Japanese as they read it. Classical Japanese texts could now be equipped with extensive *furigana* glosses for names and difficult words written in Chinese graphs. New glossed editions of older works, and the automatic provision of glosses for new works, made texts accessible to readers with middling levels of literacy and thus extended the potential market for printed books.

The market for printed books in Edo-period Japan was dominated by the vernacular, including vernacularised Chinese texts equipped with glosses. By contrast, the Japanese *hiragana* and *katakana* syllabaries were almost entirely absent from xylographic books printed before 1600. There were a few exceptions. One was *Kurodani shōnin gotōroku* 黒谷上人語燈録, which is a collection of the sermons and writings of Hōnen 法然 (1133–1212), the founder of Pure Land Buddhism in Japan, and which was printed in 1321; another contains the writings of Rennyo 蓮如 (1415–99), a monk of the True Pure Land school of Buddhism, printed in the mid-sixteenth century; and there are a few collections of sermons printed in a mixture of Chinese graphs and the Japanese *katakana* syllabary, including *Muchū mondōshū* 夢中問答集 (1344) and *Enzan wadei gassuishū* 塩山和泥合水集 (1386).[101] In addition, there are several Japanese works which were printed in literary Chinese with glosses in the *hiragana* or *katakana* syllabaries, and calendars routinely included *hiragana* text.[102] The ubiquity of the Japanese script in books and other media printed in the Edo period provides

---

[101] Nihon Shoshi Gakkai (1932), #23 and plates 43–4; Tokushi (1929), #19; Kawase (1970), 1: 357, 451.

[102] For images of these, see Kawase (1970), vol. 2, plates 508–12, 538–9.

a striking contrast with the books printed in earlier centuries, but this was not itself a product of xylography; it was, rather, a product of the vernacularisation of written culture which affected East Asian societies just as much as it did other societies.[103] Xylography did, however, facilitate the process of vernacularisation by making the glossing of Chinese texts much easier.

Finally, the revival of xylography in Japan also had long-term beneficial consequences. Firstly, it facilitated the combination of text and image on the same page, and this took various forms, from images with inserted text to small images inserted in the text and text wrapped around an image. Secondly, it stimulated the creative use of non-text elements in the *mise-en-page*, such as borders, headings and graphic devices. Thirdly, it facilitated low-cost provincial printing. This is clear from the fact that by the end of the seventeenth century a number of small-scale publishers and printers had emerged in castle towns such as Nagoya and Kanazawa.[104] However, it has to be admitted that we have no documentary evidence to make any judgement about the comparative economics of typography and xylography in seventeenth-century Japan.[105] Fourthly, it made it much easier to cater to demand that was spread over several years (sometimes in excess of 100 years) by using the same woodblocks and thus obviating the need to reset the type. As mentioned earlier, the fact that different typographic editions of the same book were frequently put out by the same publishers in a short period of time in the early Edo period shows just how hard it was to match typography with demand. Xylography eliminated that problem, and it therefore made good sense to abandon typography in favour of the tried and tested technology of xylography.

---

[103] On this topic, see Kornicki (2018).

[104] Asakura and Ōwa (1993). As Suzuki (2022) shows in the case of Zenkōji, jobbing printers were active in many provincial towns, producing advertising material, local maps and the like, so xylography had spread widely by the beginning of the nineteenth century, if not well before.

[105] Heijdra (2004a) provides some figures for the economics of printing in nineteenth-century China, but we have no way of knowing how applicable, if at all, they are to the circumstances of seventeenth-century Japan.

7 Takagi Takaaki's Argument

In 2020 the Japanese scholar Takagi Takaaki, in his magisterial study of
typography in Japan in the late sixteenth and early seventeenth centuries,
cast some doubt on the argument I have developed here, part of which I had
earlier presented in a Japanese journal.[106] Let me first give a translation of
the key passage in the book which presents the nub of his argument so that
his words can speak for themselves:

> Among old Japanese typographic editions [*kokatsujiban*],
> there are some glossed typographic editions [*fukun choku-
> hanbon*] in which small-size type is inserted between the lines
> of the text to form *furigana* (many are to be found among the
> editions printed in the early Edo period on Mt. Kōya or Mt.
> Hiei) and others in which the Chinese graph and the *fur-
> igana* form a single piece of type (mostly found in books
> with Japanese text). However, the quantity of books of this
> type does not even amount to one tenth of the total number
> of old Japanese typographic editions. The reason for that is
> sometimes said to be that it was more complicated and
> inconvenient to prepare the type for printing in such cases
> than when printing the text alone, but are such technological
> problems the real reason? It cannot be denied that an early
> instance of an old Japanese typographic edition with added
> *furigana* is the *hiragana* version of the *Taiheiki* [Record of
> great peace] printed in 1609. However, it is a fact that most
> editions with *furigana* were printed not in the Keichō [1596–
> 1615] and Genna [1615–24] eras but in the Kan'ei era [1624–
> 44]. Moreover, it is probably significant that they were not
> Chinese texts but Japanese texts. In other words, it should
> surely be considered that the presence or absence of furigana
> was a result not of technological problems but rather of the
> moment in time and the nature of the book in question. As

[106] Kornicki (2015).

I have mentioned earlier, old Japanese typographic editions of Chinese texts in particular were produced in the expectation that an appropriate person would write in, or have somebody write in, the appropriate readings. In other words, they were only complete once the readings had been written in. In that sense, old Japanese typographic editions may have been printed books, but they had the character of manuscripts. When one considers the case of the typographic edition of the *Shiji* 史記 [*Records of the grand historian*, J. *Shiki*] with *kunten* glosses added by Kan Tokuan 管得庵 [1581–1628] mentioned in the previous chapter and the fact that the first to add Japanese *kunten* glosses to the *Beixi xian sheng Xing li ẓi yi* 北渓先生性理字 [Master Beixi's *The meanings of Neo-Confucian terms*, J. *Hokkei sensei seiri jigi*] was Kan Tokuan, one feels that it is clear why numerous copies of the typographic edition of the *Qi shu jiang yi* 七書講義 [*Lectures on the seven books*, J. *Shichisho kōgi*] should have come down to us with *kunten* added by Kan Tokuan soon after publication.[107]

In this passage Takagi draws a distinction between typographic editions of Chinese texts and those of Japanese texts. He argues that technological difficulties are not at issue and that one of the key issues is the chronology, considering that practice in the 1620s and 1630s was quite different from that in the earlier period. Takagi seems to be arguing that in the 1620s and 1630s, when typography was in fact beginning to enter a decline, typographic books with Japanese text were more likely to include printed *furigana*. The problem with this argument is that, as Takagi himself points out, the numbers of such books even in the Kan'ei era (1624–44) is not large, so the question remains why the inclusion of *furigana* in typographic editions was so infrequent. In the case of Japanese texts, the argument Takagi makes about the need for authoritative readings added by an appropriate person

---

[107] Takagi (2020), 626–7. Round parentheses are Takagi's, square ones are my additions.

does not apply, and he offers no alternative explanation, so it is difficult to avoid the conclusion that, at least in the case of Japanese texts, the difficulty and inconvenience of having to provide *furigana* in typographic editions encouraged the abandonment of typography.

The case of Chinese texts is somewhat different; after all, *kunten* glosses are very different from *furigana* and require considerable sinological expertise, as Takagi rightly emphasises. He goes so far as to say that typographic editions of Chinese texts were incomplete if they lacked handwritten *kunten* glosses entered by an appropriate person such as Kan Tokuan. To be sure, in the early seventeenth century there were very few readers of Chinese texts who could cope with the raw text without the assistance provided by *kunten* glosses. Kan Tokuan (1581–1628), who had studied with the medical pioneer Manase Gensaku (mentioned earlier) and with the famous exponent of Neo-Confucianism, Fujiwara Seika, was certainly an appropriate person to add glosses in the light of his learning. But it is not clear why Takagi mentions only him: was he the only one to be asked to add glosses by hand to printed Chinese texts? Or is he the only concrete example Takagi has been able to find?

There certainly was a need for the kind of authoritative glosses that could only be provided by an appropriate person, but Takuan was not by any means the only person who could be considered appropriate. Let us consider the 1670 edition of the catalogue of books in print issued by the booksellers of Kyoto. At the beginning of the section on the Chinese classics come the *Four Books* with annotations by Zhu Xi, which indicated that the interpretations were those of the orthodox Neo-Confucian tradition. The entry in the Kyoto booksellers' catalogue for this item reveals that potential purchasers of this text in 1670 had a choice: they could buy editions with glosses provided by Nanpo Bunshi, Hayashi Razan or Yamazaki Ansai, or an edition without any glosses at all.[108] Nanpo Bunshi (1555–1620), Hayashi Razan (1583–1657) and Yamazaki Ansai (1619–82) were all prominent Neo-Confucian scholars and very definitely fell into the category of appropriate persons to provide *kunten* glosses for Chinese texts. Needless to say, all these were woodblock editions, for it

---

[108] Shidō Bunko, ed. (1962–4), 1: 77.

was only woodblock printing that afforded the possibility of including extensive *kunten* glosses with ease. It is evident from the publication of these various editions that readers needed the glosses which only eminent sinologists could provide, and it is worth noting that Kan Takuan is not amongst them, although Nanpo Bunshi, who was of the previous generation, is included. In fact, the only one of them who was still alive in 1670 was Yamazaki Ansai. From this it is clear that there was no intrinsic objection to Chinese texts being issued with printed *kunten* glosses, at least by the 1670s, provided that the glossator was a reputable sinologist. In fact, for the remainder of the Edo period, right up to the Meiji Restoration of 1868 and beyond, editions of Chinese texts routinely included *kunten* glosses by a named glossator, and sometimes a lot more than that. For example, the immensely popular *Keiten yoshi* 経典余師 (Classics without a teacher) series produced from the 1780s onwards by Tani Hyakunen (1754–1831) included reading guides and translations as well as the glossed original texts.[109]

Takagi argues that in the early part of the seventeenth century typographic editions of the Chinese classics needed to be equipped after printing with handwritten glosses by a suitable person. That may be so, but the fact that he mentions only one name does not inspire confidence, and it remains a fact that many extant typographic editions of Chinese classical texts from that period are not equipped with any glosses at all. Moreover, Takagi does not address two other categories of typographic books, namely non-canonical Chinese texts and all Japanese texts. By 'non-canonical Chinese texts' I mean texts that did not form part of the classical canon that included the *Analects*, *Mencius*, the *Book of Songs*, and so on. Medical, literary and historical texts did not belong to the classical canon and so cannot be said to have required the addition of glosses by an appropriate person so as to prevent readers from misunderstanding the text. Much the same can be said of Japanese texts like *Shoshitsu* and *Saiminki*, to say nothing of the vast number of literary, historical and other Japanese texts which were printed typographically in the early years of the seventeenth

---

[109] Suzuki (2007).

century and then printed xylographically later. Whatever may have been the case with typographic editions of canonical Chinese texts, where Takagi's argument is that *kunten* glosses needed to be added by hand by a recognised authority, that consideration did not apply to Japanese texts, which required not *kunten* glosses for comprehension but *furigana* for ease of reading and accessibility. Takagi does not suggest that *furigana* needed to be applied by appropriate people to typographic editions of Japanese texts, so my argument that it was the pressure to include *furigana* that led to the abandonment of typography surely still stands. Finally, it is worth recalling that Kawase pointed out long ago that there must have been technological dissatisfaction with the problems of trying to print illustrated books and books with *furigana* glosses typographically.[110] He did not follow this suggestion up, but he was surely pointing the way to a more persuasive explanation.

---

[110] Kawase (1967a), 1: 630.

8 Conclusion

In seventeenth-century Japan three different technologies were in use for the production of books: handwriting, xylography and typography. In addition, the supply of books in Japan was enhanced by the importation of books from the Chinese coast and from the Korean peninsula. Chinese books were imported on Chinese vessels docking at Nagasaki, while Korean books (almost all of them written in literary Chinese) were either purchased in Korea by Japanese who were resident on the island of Tsushima, which lies between Korea and Japan, and had the right to visit Korea, were donated by Koreans visiting Japan or were given by the Korean court in response to an official request from Japan. Surprisingly, in view of the recent Japanese invasion of Korea, the Korean court acceded to some of these requests. One of the most important acquisitions in the seventeenth century was the *Mirror of Eastern medicine* (K. *Tong'ŭi pogam* 東醫寶鑑). This was a medical encyclopedia which was compiled by the Korean physician Hŏ Chun 許浚 (1546–1615) and first printed, xylographically, in Korea in 1613, and it was highly regarded in both China and Japan. A copy of this work is known to have been presented by a Korean physician to his Japanese counterpart on the island of Tsushima.[111] In terms of quantity, it was imports from China that were more significant, and they enabled Japanese readers with a good knowledge of Chinese to keep abreast of intellectual and political developments in China. This proved particularly important in the mid nineteenth century, when the *Illustrated treatise on the maritime countries* (*Haiguo tuzhi* 海國圖志) brought news of the humiliating conclusion of the Opium War and warned of the dangers posed by the Western maritime powers.[112]

There were, therefore, many different types of books in circulation in seventeenth-century Japan. In addition to manuscripts, xylographic books and typographic books that were produced in Japan, there were also printed books and manuscripts imported from China and Korea. Also, via the Dutch trading station on the island of Deshima in Nagasaki, some Dutch books, including translations of books in other European

---

[111] Kornicki (2013), 81. [112] Ōba (1967); Wakabayashi (1992).

languages, were also reaching Japan, although 'Dutch learning' (Rangaku 蘭学) was only to take off as a new field of study in the second half of the eighteenth century.[113] Within this galaxy of books, the typographic editions of the early seventeenth century played a very small part, though they have attracted a great deal of attention, particularly in Japan. The fact is that the overwhelming bulk of books in circulation were either Japanese manuscripts or books printed xylographically in Japan, not typographic books.

The fact that the recently arrived technology of typography flourished for only a few decades in Japan and after that lingered at a very low level until the end of the Edo period may at first sight seem surprising to people familiar with the history of printing in Europe. However, the abandonment of typography was by no means whimsical. On the contrary, the reversion to xylography laid the foundations for the growth of commercial publishing in the remainder of the Edo period. Publishing in that period encompassed both texts in Chinese (written by Chinese, Korean or Japanese authors) and texts in Japanese, but the use of xylography enabled publishers to keep numerous works in print at the same time and to respond flexibly to demand. It also enabled editions of Chinese texts to be equipped with printed *kunten* glosses as well as commentary in smaller size and enabled Japanese texts to be provided with extensive *furigana* glosses that made them accessible to an ever wider market. As I have shown, for a brief while at the beginning of the seventeenth century brave attempts were made to incorporate such glosses typographically, but they proved to be cumbersome, they were limited in scope and they did not attact the attention of most printers. Since all these glosses, and much more, could be easily, efficiently and economically achieved with xylography, abandoning typography at that stage in Japanese history can only be described as having been a wise and rational choice.

---

[113] Boot (2009).

References

Asakura Haruhiko 朝倉治彦 and Ōwa Hiroyuki 大和博幸, eds. (1993). *Kinsei chihō shuppan no kenkyū* 近世地方出版の研究, Tōkyō: Tōkyōdō Shuppan.

Barrett, T. H. (2001a). 'Woodblock dyeing and printing technology in China, c. 700 AD: The innovations of Ms. Liu, and other evidence'. *Bulletin of the School of Oriental and African Studies* 64, 240–7.

(2001b). *The rise and spread of printing: A new account of religious factors*, London: SOAS.

(2005). 'Religion and the first recorded print run: Luoyang, July, 855'. *Bulletin of the School of Oriental and African Studies* 68, 455–61.

(2008). *The woman who discovered printing*, New Haven, CT: Yale University Press.

(2011). 'The woman who discovered notepaper: Towards a comparative historiography of paper and print'. *Journal of the Royal Asiatic Society* 21, 199–210.

Berry, M. E. (2006). *Japan in print: Information and nation in the early modern period*, Berkeley: University of California Press.

Boot, W. J. (2009). 'The transfer of learning: The import of Chinese and Dutch books in Tokugawa Japan'. In E. Groenendijk, C. Viallé and J. L. Blussé, eds., *Canton and Nagasaki compared, 1730–1830: Dutch, Chinese, Japanese relations transactions*, Leiden: IGEER, 45–56.

Bulliet, R. W. (1987). 'Medieval Arabic tarsh: A forgotten chapter in the history of printing'. *Journal of the American Oriental Society* 107, 427–38.

Burke, P., and J. P. McDermott (2015). 'Introduction'. In P. Burke and J. P. McDermott, eds., *The book worlds of East Asia and Europe, 1450–1850: Connections and comparisons*, Hong Kong: Hong Kong University Press, 1–64.

Bussotti, M., and Han Qi (2014). 'Typography for a modern world? The ways of Chinese movable types'. *East Asian Science, Technology, and Medicine* 40, 9–44.

Carter, T. F. (1955). *The invention of printing in China and its spread westward*, 2nd ed., New York: Ronald Press.

Chen Chingho 陳荊和, ed. (1984–6). *Kyōgōbon Daietsu shiki ʒensho* 校合本大越史記全書, 3 vols., Tōkyō: Tōyōgaku Bunken Sentā.

Chia, L. (2000). 'Printing and publishing in East Asia through circa 1600: An extremely brief survey'. *Mediaevalia* 41, 129–62.

Chibbett, D. (1977). *The history of Japanese printing and book illustration*, Tōkyō: Kōdansha International.

Chō Shūmin [Zhang Xiumin] 張秀民 et al. (2009). *Katsuji insatsu no bunkashi* 活字印刷の文化史, Tōkyō: Bensei Shuppan.

Choi Byonghyon (trans. and annotated) (2014). *The annals of King T'aejo, founder of Korea's Chosŏn dynasty*, Cambridge, MA: Harvard University Press.

Ch'ŏn Hyebong 千惠鳳 (1976). *Han'guk koinswaesa* 韓國古印刷史, Seoul: Han'guk Tosŏgwanhak Yŏn'guhoe.

Chosŏn wangjo sillok 朝鮮王朝實録 [references are made to reign and date]. Digital edition: https://sillok.history.go.kr/main/main.do.

Chow, Kai-wing (2004). *Publishing, culture, and power in early modern China*, Stanford, CA: Stanford University Press.

(2007). 'Reinventing Gutenberg: Woodblock and movable-type printing in Europe and China'. In S. A. Brown, E. N. Lindquist and E. T. Shevlin, eds., *Agent of change: Print culture studies after Eliʒabeth Eisenstein*, Amherst: University of Massachusetts Press, in association with the Center for the Book, Library of Congress, 169–92.

Copland, P. (1639). 'Patrick Copland to John Winthrop'. In Massachusetts Historical Society, ed., 'The Winthrop Papers' III, *Collections of the*

Massachusetts Historical Society, fifth series, vol. 1, 1871. Boston: Massachusetts Historical Society, 277–80.

Davis, J. N., and L. Chance (2016). 'The handwritten and the printed: Issues of format and medium in Japanese premodern books'. *Manuscript Studies* 1, 90–115.

Drège, J.-P. (1984). 'Les caractères de l'impératrice Wu Zetian dans les manuscrits de Dunhuang et de Turfan'. *Bullétin de l'École Française d'Extrême-Orient* 73, 339–54.

(2006). 'Le livre imprimé sino-tangut'. *Journal Asiatique* 294, 343–71.

Dunnell, R. W. (1996). *The great state of White and High: Buddhism and state formation in eleventh-century Xia*, Honolulu: University Press of Hawai'i.

Elverskog, J. (1997). *Uygur Buddhist literature*, Turnhout: Brepols.

Endō Jirō 遠藤次郎 and Nakamura Teruko 中村輝子 (2004). 'Manase Gensaku no chosaku no shomondai: *Sankyo shiyō bassui*, *Saiminki* wa Gensaku no chosaku ka' 曲直瀬玄朔の著作の諸問題：『山居四要抜粋』『済民記』は玄朔の著作か. *Nihon ishigaku zasshi* 日本医史学雑誌 50, 547–68.

Farrington, A. (1991). *The English factory in Japan: 1613–1623*, London: The British Library.

Farrington, J. (2001). 'The first twelve voyages of the English East India Company, 1601–13: A guide to sources'. *Indonesia and the Malay World* 29:85, 141–60.

Fitzgerald, D. (2024). 'A global experiment in printing: The circulation of the Nestorian Stele from Xi'an'. In S. J. Campbell and S. Porras, eds., *The Routledge companion to global Renaissance art*, London: Routledge, 177–89.

Forrer, M. (1985). *Eirakuya Tōshirō, publisher at Nagoya*, Uithoorn: J. C. Gieben.

Fukuzawa Yukichi (2007). *The autobiography of Fukuzawa Yukichi*, revised translation by E. Kiyooka, New York: Columbia University Press.

Galambos, I. (2015). *Translating Chinese tradition and teaching Tangut culture: Manuscripts and printed books from Khara-Khoto*, Berlin: De Gruyter.

Gardner, K. B. (1993). *Descriptive catalogue of Japanese books in the British Library printed before 1700*, London: British Library; Tenri: Tenri Central Library.

González-Bolado, J. (2023). 'Two unpublished letters on the Jesuit Mission Press in late sixteenth-century Japan'. *East Asian Publishing and Society* 13, 37–46.

Gotō Kenji 後藤憲二 (2003). *Kan'eiban shomoku narabi ni zuhan* 寛永版書目並図版, Higashi-Murayama: Seishōdō Shoten.

Hayashi, N., and P. Kornicki (1991). *Early Japanese books in Cambridge University Library: A catalogue of the Aston, Satow and von Siebold collections*, Cambridge: Cambridge University Press.

Heijdra, M. J. (2004a). 'The development of modern typography in East Asia, 1850–2000'. *East Asian Library Journal* 11:2, 100–68.

(2004b). 'Technology, culture and economics: Moveable type versus woodblock printing in East Asia'. In Isobe Akira, ed., *Studies of publishing culture in East Asia – Niwatazumi*, Tōkyō: Nigensha, 223–40.

Hickman, B. (1975). 'A note on the Hyakumantō Dhāranī'. *Monumenta Nipponica* 30, 87–93.

Hiranaka Reiji 平中苓次 (1967). 'Chōsen kokatsujibon *Hanjo* ni tsuite' 朝鮮古活字本漢書について. In Hiranaka Reiji, *Chūgoku kodai no densei to zeihō: Shin-Kan keizaishi kenkyū* 中國古代の田制と税法: 秦漢經濟史研究, Tōyōshi Kenkyūkai.

Hokkekyō onkun 法華経音訓 (1931). Facsimile edition, Kyoto: Kichō Tosho Eiin Kankōkai.

Hou, H. (2017). 'Notes on the translation and transmission of the Saṃpuṭa and Cakrasaṃvara Tantras in the Xixia period (1038–1227)'. In Y. Bentor and M. Shahar, eds., *Chinese and Tibetan Esoteric Buddhism*, Leiden: Brill, 355–76.

Hu Daojing 胡道静, ed. (2012). *Xin jiao zheng Mengxi bitan* 新校證夢溪筆談, Shanghai: Shanghai Renmin Chubanshe.

Hu Daojing, Jin Liangnian 金良年 and Hu Xiaojing 胡小静 (trans. into modern Chinese), Wang Hong 王宏 and Zhao Zheng 赵峥 (trans. into English) (2008). *Mengxi bitan Brush talks from a dream book*, Chengdu: Sichuan Renmin Chubanshe.

Ichinohe Wataru 一戸涉 (2019). 'Matsudaira Sadanobu no *Ise monogatari* hissha katsudō to sono shūhen' 松平定信の伊勢物語筆写活動とその周辺. *Kokubungaku Kenkyū Shiryōkan chōsa hōkoku* 39, 49–61.

Inoue Susumu 井上進 (2011). *Min Shin gakujutsu hensenshi: shuppan to dentō gakujutsu no rinkaiten* 明清学術変遷史：出版と伝統学術の臨界点, Tōkyō: Heibonsha.

Kawase Kazuma 川瀬一馬 (1967a). *(Zōho) Kokatsujiban no kenkyū* 増補古活字版之研究, Tōkyō: The Antiquarian Booksellers Association of Japan.

　　(1967b). 'Baijuken no isho kaihan ni tsuite' 梅壽軒の医書開版につて. *Shoshigaku* 9, 1–20.

　　(1970). *Gozanban no kenkyū* 五山版の研究, Tōkyō: Nihon Koshosekishō Kyōkai.

Kim Sŏngsu 金聖洙 (2000). *Mugu chŏngguang tae t'arani kyŏng ŭi yŏngu* 無垢浄光大陀羅尼経의研究, Ch'ŏngju: Ch'ŏngju Koinswae Pangmulgwan.

　　(2007). '*Mugu chŏngguang tae t'arani kyŏng* ŭi kanhaeng sigi e kwanhan chaegŏmjŭng yŏngu' 무구정광대다라니경의 간행시기에 관한 재검증 연구. *Sŏjihak yŏngu* 書誌學研究 36, 39–79.

　　(2013). 'Han'guk kŭmsok hwalja siwŏn ŭi wŏnch'ŏn kisul mit Hŭngdŏksa-ja chujobŏp e kwanhan yŏn'gu' 한국 금속활자 始原의 원천기술 및 興德寺字의 鑄造法에 관한 연구. *Sŏjihak yŏn'gu* 54, 75–102.

Kinoshita, K. (2000). 'The advent of movable-type printing: The early Keichō period and Kyoto Cultural Circles'. In F. Fischer, ed., *The Arts* of Hon'ami Kōetsu, Japanese Renaissance Master, Philadelphia, PA: Philadelphia Museum of Art, 56–73.

Kishimoto Masami 岸本真実 (1985). 'Jōōki mokkatsujibon *Shōgaku* ni tsuite' 承応期木活字本「小学」について. *Biburia* 85, 64–72.

(1986). 'Kinsei mokkatsujiban gaikan' 近世木活字版概観. *Biburia* 87, 72–94.

Koakimoto Dan 小秋元段 (2021). 'Sagabon to sono zenshi no ichisōbō' 嵯峨本とその前史の一相貌. *Hōsei Daigaku Bungakubu kiyō* 法政大学文学部紀要 82, 21–37.

Kornicki, P. F. (2006). 'Manuscript, not print: Scribal culture in the Edo period'. *Journal of Japanese Studies* 32, 23–52.

(2008). 'Books in the service of politics: Tokugawa Ieyasu as custodian of the books of Japan'. *Journal of the Royal Asiatic Society* 18, 71–82.

(2012). 'The Hyakumantō Darani and the origins of printing in eighth-century Japan'. *International Journal of Asian Studies* 9, 1–28.

(2013). 'Korean books in Japan: From the 1590s to the end of the Edo period'. *Journal of the American Oriental Society* 133, 71–92.

(2015). 'Fukun katsujibon *Shoshitsu kinkōshū* to Baiju no shuppan katsudō: kokatsujiban shūen no kaimei ni mukete' 附訓活字本『諸疾禁好集』と梅壽の出版活動 ―― 古活字版終焉の解明にむけて. *Biburia* 144, 1–17.

(2018). *Languages, scripts, and Chinese texts in East Asia*, Oxford: Oxford University Press.

(2019). 'Edo jidai shoki shuppan nenpyō kaigaiban' 江戸時代初期出版年表海外版. *Kokubungaku Kenkyū Shiryōkan Chōsa kenkyū hōkoku* 39, 263–93.

Kuboo Toshirō 久保尾俊郎 (2008). 'Ishibe-shi no kankō jigyō' 石部氏の刊行事業. *Waseda Daigaku Toshokan Kiyō* 55, 29–47.

Lê Quí Đôn 黎貴惇 (2011). *Vân đài loại ngữ* 芸薹類語. In *Dong ya ruxue ziliao congshu* 東亞儒學資料叢書 vol. 7, Taibei: Guoli Taiwan Daxue Chuban Zhongxin.

Lee Hee-Jae (1987). *La typographie coréenne au XVe siècle*, Paris: Editions CNRS.

Lee, P. H., ed., (1993–6). *Sourcebook of Korean civilization*, 2 vols., New York: Columbia University Press.

Liu Yujun 劉玉珺 (2005). 'Yuenan guji kanke shulun' 越南古籍刊刻述論. *Yuwai hanji yanjiu jikan* 域外漢籍研究集刊 1, 269–92.

Loureiro, R. M. (2006). 'Kirishitan Bunko: Alessandro Valignano and the Christian press in Japan'. *Revista de cultura* 19, 135–53.

Lurie, D. B. (2011). *Realms of literacy: Early Japan and the history of writing*, Cambridge, MA: Harvard University Asia Center.

Macouin, F. (1986). 'A propos de caractères d'imprimerie ouïgours'. In J.-P. Drège, M. Ishigami-Iagolnitzer, and M. Cohen, eds, *Le livre et l'imprimerie en extreme-orient et en Asie du Sud*, Bordeaux: Société Bibliophiles de Guyenne, 147–56.

Magnússon, S. G. (2017). *Minor knowledge and microhistory: Manuscript culture in the nineteenth century*, Abingdon: Routledge.

McDermott, J. P. (2006). *A Social history of the Chinese book: Books and literati in late imperial China*, Hong Kong: Hong Kong University Press.

Miyagawa Yōko 宮川葉子 (2006). 'Rakuō to *Genji monogatari*' 楽翁と『源氏物語』. *Bungaku* 7:1, 140–51.

Mizukami Fumiyoshi 水上文義 (2002). 'Tenkaiban issaikyō mokkatsuji no tokushoku' 天海版一切経木活字の特色. *Indogaku bukkyōgaku kenkyū* 101, 209–13.

Moran, J. F. (1993). *The Japanese and the Jesuits: Alessandro Valignano in sixteenth-century Japan*, London: Routledge.

Moretti, L. (2012). 'The Japanese early-modern publishing market unveiled: A survey of Edo-period booksellers' catalogues'. *East Asian Publishing and Society* 2: 199–308.

Nakane Katsu 中根勝 (1999). *Nihon insatsu gijutsu shi* 日本印刷技術史, Tōkyō: Yagi Shoten.

Nakano Mitsutoshi 中野三敏 (1995). *Shoshigaku dangi: Edo no hanpon* 書誌学談義;江戸の板本, Tōkyō: Iwanami Shoten.

Nihon Shoshi Gakkai 日本書誌學會, ed. (1932). *Kyūkan eifu* 舊刊景譜, Tōkyō: Nihon Shoshi Gakkai.

Niu Dasheng 牛达生 (2004). *Xixia huoẓi yinshua yanjiu* 西夏活字印刷研究, Yinchuan: Ningxia Renmin Chubanshe.

Ōba Osamu 大庭脩 (1967). *Edo jidai ni okeru tōsen mochiwatashisho no kenkyū* 江戸時代における唐船持渡書の研究, Suita: Kansai Daigaku Tōzai Gakujutsu Kenkyūsho.

Oka Masahiko 岡雅彦 et al., comp. (2011). *Edo jidai shoki shuppan nenpyō: Tenshō jūkunen – Meireki yonen* 江戸時代初期出版年表－天正十九年〜明暦四年, Tōkyō: Bensei Shuppan.

Okajima Ikuko 岡嶌偉久子 (1997). 'Matsudaira Sadanobu jihitsu *Imawa no koi: Genji monogatari* no shosha nikki' 松平定信自筆『今波恋』(1) － 源氏物語の書写日記. *Biburia* 107, 100–33; 108, 340–73.

Ōuchida Sadao 大内田貞郎 (2000). 'Kokatsujiban no rūtsu, soshite shūen (shōmetsu)' 古活字版」のルーツ, そして終焉(消滅). *Biburia* 113, 23–39.

(2009). 'Kirishitanban ni kokatsujiban no rūtsu o saguru' 「きりした ん版」に「古活字版」のルーツを探る. In Chō Shūmin [Zhang Xiumin] 張秀民 et al., *Katsuji insatsu no bunkashi* 活字印刷の文化史：きりしたん版・古活字版から新常用漢字表まで, Tōkyō, Bensei Shuppan, 19–68.

Pan Jixing (1997). 'On the origin of printing in the light of new archae-ological discoveries'. *Chinese Science Bulletin* 42.12, 976–81.

潘吉星 (2009). *Zhongguo ʐaoji shi* 中国造纸史, Shanghai: Shanghai Renmin Chubanshe.

Parshall, P., and R. Schoch, eds. (2005). *Origins of European printmaking: Fifteenth-century woodcuts and their public*, New Haven, CT: Yale University Press.

Richardson, K. (2022). *Roma in the medieval Islamic world: Literacy, culture, and migration*, London: I. B. Tauris.

Robb, M. E. (2020). *Print and the Urdu public: Muslims, newspapers, and urban life in Colonial India*, Oxford: Oxford University Press.

Robinson, F. (1993). 'Technology and religious change: Islam and the impact of print'. *Modern Asian Studies* 27, 229–51.

Sasaki Takahiro 佐々木孝浩 (2016). 'Kirishitanban kokujitai no zōhon ni tsuite: hiragana kokatsujibon to no hikaku o tōshite' キリシタン版国字本の造本について : 平仮名古活字本との比較を通して. *Shidō Bunko ronshū* 斯道文庫論集 51, 33–61.

   trans. M. Burtscher (2022). 'Jesuit printing and Hiragana books'. *Monumenta Nipponica* 77, 27–75.

Schaefer, K. R. (2006). *Enigmatic charms: Medieval Arabic block printed amulets in American and European libraries and museums*, Leiden: Brill.

   (2014). 'Mediaeval Arabic block printing: The state of the field'. In G. Roper, ed., *Historical aspects of printing and publishing in languages of the Middle East: Papers from the Third Symposium on the History of Printing and Publishing in the Languages and Countries of the Middle East, University of Leipʐig, September 2008*, Leiden: Brill, 1–16.

Seo Tatsuhiko (2003). 'The publishing industry in Chang'an's eastern market in the Tang dynasty'. *Memoirs of the Toyo Bunko* 6, 1–42.

   妹尾達彦 (2009). 'Tōdai Chōan no insatsu bunka: omo ni S.P.12 o tegakari ni shite' 唐代長安の印刷文化−主にS.P.12とS.P.6を手がかりに−. In Dohi Yoshikazu 土肥義和, ed., *Tonkō Torufan*

shutsudo kanbun monjo no shinkenkyū 敦煌・吐魯番出土漢文文書
の新研究, *Tōyō Bunko ronsō* 東洋文庫論叢 72, 427–46.

Shi Jinbo 史金波 and Yasen Wushou'er 雅森・吾守尔 (2000). *Zhongguo huoʐi yinshua shu de faming he ʐaoqi chuanbo: Xi Xia he Huihu huo ʐi yinshuashu yanjiu* 中国活字印刷术的发明和早期传播：西夏和回鹘活字印刷术研究, Beijing: Shehui Kexue Wenxian Chubanshe.

Shidō Bunko 斯道文庫, ed. (1962–64). *(Edo jidai) Shorin shuppan shojaku mokuroku shūsei* 江戸時代書林出版書籍目録集成, 4 vols., Tōkyō: Shidō Bunko.

Shockey, N. (2019) *The typographic imagination: Reading and writing in Japan's age of modern print media*, New York: Columbia University Press.

Sivin, N. (2015). 'Recent publications on Shen Kuo's *Menxi bitan* (Brush talks from dream brook)'. *East Asian Science, Technology, and Medicine*, 42, 93–102.

Son Pogi [Sohn Pow-key] 孫寶基 (1987). *Han'guk ŭi kohwalja* 한국의 고활자, new edition, Seoul: Pojinjae.

Sorimachi Shigeo 反町茂雄 (1972). *Kōbunsō kokatsujiban mokuroku* 弘文莊古活字版目録, Tōkyō: Kōbunsō.

Suh, S. (2020). *Naming the local: Medicine, language, and identity in Korea since the fifteenth century*, Leiden: Brill.

Steininger, B. (2018). 'Manuscript culture and Chinese learning in medieval Kamakura'. *Harvard Journal of Asiatic Studies* 78, 339–69.

(2019). 'The scribal imaginary in medieval Japanese paratexts', *Journal of Japanese Studies* 45, 241–67.

Sun Shouling (2007). 'Why I reprinted the final portion of the Vimilakīrti-nirdeśa using moveable type made of clay', trans. A. D. Smith, annotated by L. von Falkenhausen. *Early Medieval China* 13–14, 233–63.

Suzuki, J., E. Tinios and R. J. Ruben (2013). *Understanding Japanese woodblock-printed illustrated books: A short introduction to their history, bibliography and format*, Leiden: Brill.

Suzuki Toshiyuki 鈴木俊幸 (2007). *Edo no dokushonetsu: jigaku suru dokusha to shoseki ryūtsū* 江戸の読書熱：自学する読者と書籍流通, Tōkyō: Heibonsha.

(2022). 'Mokuhan insatsu no yukue: Shinshū Zenkōjimachi no baai' 木版印刷のゆくえ—信州善光寺町の場合. *Shomotsugaku* 書物学 21, 4–9.

Tajihi Ikuo 多治比郁夫 (2007). 'Baijuken no fukunkoku seihanbon' 梅寿軒の附訓刻整版本. In 'Chōsa yoroku' 調査余録, *Keihan bungei shiryō* 京阪文芸史料, vol. 5, Higashi-Murayama: Seishōdō Shoten, 676–82.

Tajihi Ikuo 多治比郁夫 and Nakano Mitsutoshi 中野三敏 (1990). *Kinsei katsujiban mokuroku* 近世活字版目録, Higashi-Murayama: Seishōdō Shoten.

Takagi Takaaki (2020). *Chūkinsei ikōki no bunka to kokatsujiban* 中近世移行期の文化と古活字版, Tōkyō: Bensei Shuppan.

Tenri Toshokan 天理図書館, ed. (1973). *Kirishitanban no kenkyū* きりしたん版の研究, Tenri: Tenri Daigaku Shuppanbu.

Tokiwa Daijō 常盤大定 (1936). 'Bushū shinji no ichi kenkyū' 武周新字の一研究. *Tōhō Gakuhō* 東方学報 6, 5–42.

Tokushi Yūshō 禿氏祐祥 (1929). *Koshi ẓan'yō* 古梓殘葉, np: Sugita Chōtarō.

Tōkyō Daigaku Shiryō Hensanjo 東京大學史料編纂所, ed. (1978–80). *Igirisu shōkanchō nikki* イギリス商館長日記, genbunhen 原文編, 3 vols, Tōkyō: Tōkyō Daigaku shuppankai.

Tsiang, K. R. (2010). 'Buddhist printed images and texts of the eighth-tenth centuries: Typologies of replication and representation'. In M. T. Kapstein and S. van Schaik, eds., *Esoteric Buddhism at Dunhuang: Rites and teachings for this life and beyond*, Leiden: Brill, 201–52.

Tsien Tsuen-hsuin (1985). *Paper and printing, science and civiliẓation in China vol. 5: 'Chemistry and chemical technology'*, Part 1, Cambridge: Cambridge University Press.

Ueda Yukimi 上田由紀美 (2023). 'Mukanki kokatsujiban *Mōshi*, *Shunjū Kyōden Shikkai* ga Eizanban de aru koto: yūkanki Eizan kokatsujiban *Kachū Myōhō Rengekyō*, *Shikan Girei Zuishaku* to no katsuji kumihan shuhō no kyōtsūten kara' 無刊記古活字版『毛詩』『春秋経伝集解』が叡山版であること——有刊記叡山古活字版『科註妙法蓮華経』『止観義例随釈』との活字・組版手法の共通性から——. *Kokubungaku Kenkyū Shiryōkan Chōsa Kenkyū Hōkoku* 43, 81–91.

Volker, T. (1949). *Ukiyoe quartet: Publisher, designer, engraver and printer*, Leiden: Brill.

Wakabayashi, B. T. (1992). 'Opium, expulsion, sovereignty: China's lessons for Bakumatsu Japan'. *Monumenta Nipponica* 47, 1–25.

Wood, F. (2010). *The diamond sutra: The story of the world's earliest dated printed book*, London: British Library.

Xiao Dongfa 肖东发 (1996). *Zhongguo bianji chubanshi* 中国编辑出版史, Shenyang: Liaoning jiaoyu chubanshe.

Yamada Tadao 山田忠雄 (1984). *Setsuyōshū Tenshō jūhachinenbonrui no kenkyū* 節用集天正十八年本類の研究, Tōkyō: Tōyō Bunko.

Yamamoto Tatsurō (1999). 'Development of moveable type printing in Vietnam under the Lê dynasty: A study of the comparative history between Japan and Vietnam'. *Memoirs of the Research Department of the Toyo Bunko* 57, 1–11.

Zhang Xiumin (2009). *The history of Chinese printing*, revised by Han Qi, trans. by Chen Jiehua, Chen Fu, Xu Ying, Liu Yuping, and Liu Chun. Paramus, NJ: Homa & Sekey Books.

Acknowledgements

This book is a much expanded version of an essay which was awarded the Gordon Duff Prize at the University of Cambridge in 2022. It was mostly written at the University of Chicago while I was resident as the Hanna Holborn Gray Visiting Professor in Paleography and the History of the Book.

Cambridge Elements ≡

Publishing and Book Culture

SERIES EDITOR
Samantha J. Rayner
University College London

Samantha J. Rayner is Professor of Publishing and Book
Cultures at UCL. She is also Director of UCL's Centre for
Publishing, co-Director of the Bloomsbury CHAPTER
(Communication History, Authorship, Publishing, Textual
Editing and Reading) and co-Chair of the Bookselling
Research Network.

ASSOCIATE EDITOR
Leah Tether
University of Bristol

Leah Tether is Professor of Medieval Literature and
Publishing at the University of Bristol. With an academic
background in medieval French and English literature and
a professional background in trade publishing, Leah has
combined her expertise and developed an international
research profile in book and publishing history from
manuscript to digital.

ABOUT THE SERIES

This series aims to fill the demand for easily accessible, quality texts available for teaching and research in the diverse and dynamic fields of Publishing and Book Culture. Rigorously researched and peer-reviewed Elements will be published under themes, or 'Gatherings'. These Elements should be the first check point for researchers or students working on that area of publishing and book trade history and practice: we hope that, situated so logically at Cambridge University Press, where academic publishing in the UK began, it will develop to create an unrivalled space where these histories and practices can be investigated and preserved.

Cambridge Elements ☰

Publishing and Book Culture

Publishing and Book History

Gathering Editor: Andrew Nash

Andrew Nash is Reader in Book History and Director of the London Rare Books School at the Institute of English Studies, University of London. He has written books on Scottish and Victorian Literature, and edited or co-edited numerous volumes including, most recently, *The Cambridge History of the Book in Britain, Volume 7* (Cambridge University Press, 2019).

Gathering Editor: Leah Tether

Leah Tether is Professor of Medieval Literature and Publishing at the University of Bristol. With an academic background in medieval French and English literature and a professional background in trade publishing, Leah has combined her expertise and developed an international research profile in book and publishing history from manuscript to digital.

ELEMENTS IN THE GATHERING

Publication and the Papacy in Late Antique and Medieval Europe
Samu Niskanen

Publishing in Wales: Renaissance and Resistance
Jacob D. Rawlins

The People of Print: Seventeenth-Century England
Rachel Stenner, Kaley Kramer and Adam James Smith et al.

Publishing in a Medieval Monastery: The View from Twelfth-Century Engelberg
Benjamin Pohl

Communicating the News in Early Modern Europe
Jenni Hyde, Massimo Rospocher, Joad Raymond, Yann Ryan,
Hannu Salmi and Alexandra Schäfer-Griebel

Printing Technologies and Book Production in Seventeenth-Century Japan
Peter Kornicki

A full series listing is available at: www.cambridge.org/EPBC

Printed in the United States
by Baker & Taylor Publisher Services